Volumes in This Series

Reports

1. *A Survey of Sardis and the Major Monuments outside the City Walls,* by George M. A. Hanfmann and Jane C. Waldbaum (1975)
2. *Sculpture from Sardis: The Finds through 1975,* by George M. A. Hanfmann and Nancy H. Ramage (1978)

Monographs

1. *Byzantine Coins,* by George E. Bates (1971)
2. *Ancient Literary Sources on Sardis,* by John G. Pedley (1972)
3. *Neue epichorische Schriftzeugnisse aus Sardis,* by Roberto Gusmani (1975)
4. *Byzantine and Turkish Sardis,* by Clive Foss (1976)
5. *Lydian Houses and Architectural Terracottas,* by Andrew Ramage (1978)

ARCHAEOLOGICAL EXPLORATION
OF SARDIS

General Editors

Monograph 5

Fogg Art Museum of Harvard University
Cornell University
Corning Museum of Glass
Sponsored by the American Schools
of Oriental Research

George M. A. Hanfmann
Stephen W. Jacobs
Jane Ayer Scott

Catalogue numbers **2, 14, 19, 43**

LYDIAN HOUSES AND ARCHITECTURAL TERRACOTTAS

Andrew Ramage

Harvard University Press
Cambridge, Massachusetts
London, England   1978

Library of Congress Cataloging in Publication Data

Ramage, Andrew.
   Lydian houses and architectural terracottas.
   (Monograph—Archaeological exploration of Sardis; 5)
   Bibliography: p.
   Includes index.
   1. Architecture, Domestic—Lydia. 2. Decoration
and ornament, Architectural—Lydia. 3. Terra-cotta
sculpture—To 500—Lydia. 4. Lydia. I. Title.
II. Series: Archaeological exploration of Sardis.
Monograph; 5.
NA251.L9R35   728.3'09392'2   78-15507
ISBN 0-674-53959-1

CONTENTS

EDITORS' PREFACE

The Archaeological Exploration of Sardis has been conducted since 1958 as a joint effort of the Fogg Art Museum, Harvard University, of Cornell University, and of the Corning Museum of Glass, a participant since 1960. The development of the project greatly benefited from the sponsorship of the American Schools of Oriental Research. An informal survey of the history of the project may be found in G. M. A. Hanfmann, *Letters from Sardis*. The results obtained by this collaborative effort from 1958 to 1975 are being published in two forms. The final Reports, the second of which appeared in 1978, contain the evidence from each excavated sector, accounts of major architectural monuments, and certain categories of excavated objects; the Monographs are devoted to special subjects and finds.

Because the reconstruction of the culture of Lydia is the prime objective of our archaeological work at her capital, it is a particular pleasure to welcome the first of the Monographs devoted solely to Lydian materials. Andrew Ramage of Cornell University, a member of the Expedition since 1965, presents a survey and synthesis of major traits of domestic Lydian architecture and integrates the attractive painted, mold-made architectural terracottas found at Sardis into the framework of the buildings they adorned and the stratigraphy which provides a securely dated sequence. The volume contains results of major importance both for the development of vernacular architecture and for the dating of terracottas. We are grateful to Diana C. Kamilli for her valuable analysis of clay bodies and slips.

We take this opportunity to express our profound gratitude to the government of the Republic of Turkey for the privilege of working at Sardis. The Department of Antiquities and Museums, formerly under the Ministry of the Prime Minister and now under the Ministry of Culture, and the Directors General, their officers, and representatives of the department have been unfailing in their help. We want to thank particularly the present Director General, Hikmet Gurçay, who has been a friend of the Sardis Expedition for many years.

In connection with this volume we owe a special debt to the successive directors of the Archaeological Museum, Manisa, Kemal Ziya Polatkan and Kubilây Nayır, and their staff, who have cooperated at every juncture and have assisted us by making items in storage available for study and photography.

The excavation and study of this material have been made possible by grants and contributions extending over two decades from the Bollingen Foundation (1959–1965), the Old Dominion Foundation (1966–1968), the Loeb Classical Library Foundation (1965–1970), the Wenner Gren Foundation for Anthropological Work (1967), the Charles E. Merrill Trust (1973), the Ford Foundation (1968–1972), and the Billy Rose Foundation (1970–   ). Donations were also received through the American Schools of Oriental Research. The Corning Museum of Glass made annual grants from 1960 through 1972, and Cornell University contributed university funds from 1957 through 1968. Much of the Harvard contribution came from the group of Supporters of Sardis, established in 1957, which includes both individuals and foundations. We owe the continuity of our work to their enthusiasm and generosity, and particularly to the advice and support of James R. Cherry, Landon T. Clay, Catherine S.

Detweiler, John B. Elliott, Mrs. George C. Keiser, Thomas B. Lemann, and Norbert Schimmel.

The excavation of the sectors which provide the backbone of material on which this study is based benefited from a grant in Turkish currency made by the Department of State to the President and Fellows of Harvard College for the years 1962 through 1965.[1]

A series of research grants from the National Endowment for the Humanities, largely on a matching basis, has, since 1967, played a key role in sustaining the Sardis program, and is here gratefully acknowledge.[2] Our special gratitude goes to a number of friends and foundations who in recent years have participated in the matching grants of the National Endowment for the Humanities. Travel funds for the author to complete the fieldwork in 1974 and a large portion of the costs of illustrations and records upon which this study was based were provided through the Endowment grants. In accordance with its wishes, we state that the findings and conclusions presented here do not necessarily represent the views of the Endowment.

At the Sardis research facility at Harvard, the preparation of this volume was supervised by J. A. Scott, who also provided the layout of illustrations. The drawings were prepared for publication by Elizabeth Wahle and the photographs are largely the work of Elizabeth Gombosi. Electra D. Yorsz edited the manuscript. The index was compiled by Debra A. Hudak, who also assisted with the proofreading.

We join Andrew Ramage in thanking the Hull Memorial Publications Fund of Cornell University for subsidizing publication of this volume.

1. No. SCC 29 543, under the Mutual Educational and Cultural Act, Public Law 87-256, and Agricultural Trade Development and Assistance Act, Public Law 480 as amended.

2. Grant nos. H67-0-56, H68-0-61, H69-0-23, R0-111-70-3966, R0-4999-71-171, R0-6435-72-264, R0-8359-73-217, R0-10405-74-319, R0-23511-76-541.

George M. A. Hanfmann
Jane Ayer Scott
Harvard University

Stephen W. Jacobs
Cornell University

AUTHOR'S PREFACE

This study is the result of continuous engagement with the Lydians and their buildings since my first fieldwork at Sardis in 1965. The account of Lydian domestic buildings is an outgrowth of my doctoral dissertation, and the catalogue and analysis of the architectural terracottas is a logical addition. Domestic building such as that covered in the first section is rarely treated; descriptions of housing from the archaic period are especially rare. The terracottas published in the second part are a significant addition to the corpus of architectural terracottas from Asia Minor gathered most recently by Åke Åkerström. I have, however, concentrated on the specific aspects of our material which offer opportunities for differences of interpretation and dating, and have not repeated his basic discussion of the subject.

The description of Lydian building is purposely generalized to give an overview rather than an exhaustive account of every structure excavated. In some respects it should be regarded as preliminary to what will appear in the final reports of the sectors concerned, where it is proposed to integrate the description of the buildings with that of their contents in more detail.

The catalogue of architectural terracottas is meant to present detailed accounts of individual pieces from Sardis for the use of others who are interested in this class of artifact. This group should begin to put the study of architectural terracottas on a new basis. A sequence anchored by finds from excavated contexts can integrate the techniques and methods of archaeology with those of the history of art. I have tried to indicate a date for the individual terracottas in the catalogue and, although many of them are vague, I preferred to indicate my opinion as a basis for discussion rather than to evade the issue. In most cases the date should be taken as approximate, either because the circumstances of finding do not allow greater precision or because one type or another may have been used for a considerable time. Where I do have good reason to be more precise, I try to lay out the basis for my opinion. In some cases I think that further study of the stratigraphy, in the course of preparing the final excavation reports, will narrow the dating even further.

Grid references have been included with all the pieces, although some pieces have been given approximate locations as translations of even more subjective descriptions of their findspots. This is frequently the case when things are not found in the course of the excavations. It nevertheless seemed useful to include a findspot in a uniform way if only to indicate the wide distribution at the site.

While writing this book I have benefited greatly from the advice of my mentors and colleagues on the excavations at Sardis: G. M. A. Hanfmann, C. H. Greenewalt, Jr., D. G. Mitten, and the late G. F. Swift, Jr., who started me on my investigations into Lydian building. I should also like to acknowledge the support of the National Endowment for the Humanities which underwrote my travel expenses in 1973 (under grant no. R0-8359-73-217 to the Sardis Expedition), when I was first able to study the pieces all together in the field. In addition, the Hull Memorial Publication Fund of Cornell University has assisted in the publication of this volume. I owe many thanks to the Director and staff of the Manisa Museum, especially Kubelây Nayır and Attila Tulga, who made several pieces in their keeping freely available to me. I am also very grateful to C. E. Östenberg, who discussed some of his discoveries at Acquarossa with me, and to R. Ross Holloway, who made many helpful suggestions for improving both the substance and the clarity of the manuscript. I have had many fruitful conversations on the decorative techniques and methods of production with E. Hostetter, who is at present wrestling with practical problems of making facsimiles with materials and methods available to the ancient Lydians.

For the final form of the book the editorial staff of the Sardis Research Office, particularly J. A. Scott, E. Yorsz, E. Wahle, and E. Gombosi, deserves especial thanks for patient help with the text and the illustrations. I also owe a great debt to my wife, Nancy, for her help in getting the drawings ready for publication, her persistent prodding, and patient encouragement.

Andrew Ramage
Ithaca, New York
April 1978

Technical Abbreviations

C (preceding numeral)	coin	Munsell	Soil color charts produced by Munsell Color Company, Inc. (Baltimore, Md. 1971), for color abbreviations and equivalents
ca.	circa		
C.	century		
cm.	centimeters		
D.	depth		
diam.	diameter		
E	east	N	north
esp.	especially	NoEx (preceding numeral)	Not from the excavations
est.	estimated	P (preceding numeral)	pottery
ft.	feet	P.diam.	preserved diameter
G (preceding numeral)	glass	P.H.	preserved height
H.	height	P.L.	preserved length
IN (preceding numeral)	inscription	P.W.	preserved width
km.	kilometer	r.	right
L (preceding numeral)	lamp	S	south
L.	length	S (preceding numeral)	sculpture
l.	left	T (preceding numeral)	terracotta
M (preceding numeral)	metal	Th.	thickness
m.	meters	W	west
max.	maximum	W.	width
mm.	millimeters	* (preceding numeral)	level (e.g. *98.00)

Sector Abbreviations

For a complete listing of Sardis sectors see *Sardis* R1 (1975) 13–16, for site plan see Fig. 2.

AcN	N spur of Acropolis	BNH	North apsidal hall of central part of B
AcT	Top of Acropolis		
B	Building B, the Gymnasium complex	HoB	House of Bronzes and Lydian Trench area
BE	Eastern area of B	MC	Marble Court, E of Gymnasium
BE-H	Hall with pool W of MC		
BE-N	Room N of MC	NEW	Northeast Wadi
BE-S	Room S of MC	Pa	Palaestra, E of Marble Court
BS E 1–E 19	Byzantine Shops, east shops numbers 1 through 19	PC	Pactolus Cliff area
		PN	Pactolus North area
BS W 1–W 16	Byzantine Shops, west shops numbers 1 through 16	PN/E	Church E at PN
		PN/EA	Church EA at PN
		Syn	Synagogue, S of Pa
BSH	South apsidal hall of central part of B	TU	Acropolis Tunnels

SELECTED
BIBLIOGRAPHY
AND
ABBREVIATIONS

Abbreviations of periodicals used throughout are those listed in the *American Journal of Archaeology* 80 (1975) 3–8. Abbreviations of classical authors generally follow the scheme set forth in the *Oxford Classical Dictionary,* 2nd rev. ed., N. G. L. Hammond and H. H. Scullard (Oxford 1970) ix–xxii.

The monographs and reports published by the Harvard-Cornell Expedition are cited under *Sardis,* below. The reports of the first Sardis expedition were published under the general series title of Sardis, Publications of the American Society for the Excavation of Sardis. Seventeen volumes were planned by H. C. Butler, Director of Excavations (*Sardis* I [1922] viii); of these, nine were actually published and are cited here under *Sardis.*

All publications preceding the first Sardis expedition will be found in the prospective *Bibliography of Sardis* (available in mimeographed form from the Sardis Expedition, Fogg Art Museum, Harvard University). A preliminary selection appears in Hanfmann, *Letters,* 346–349. Reports of the current expedition have appeared regularly since 1959 in the *Bulletin of the American Schools of Oriental Research* and *Türk Arkeoloji Dergisi* of the Turkish Department of Antiquities.

AH   P. Arias, M. Hirmer, and B. Shefton *A History of a Thousand Years of Greek Vase Painting* (New York 1961).

Andrén   A. Andrén *Architectural Terracottas from Etrusco-Italic Temples* (Lund 1939).

ATK   A. Åkerström *Die architektonischen Terrakotten Kleinasiens* (Lund 1966).

BASOR   *Bulletin of the American Schools of Oriental Research,* followed by volume number, then page references.

BMC Attica   B. V. Head *Catalogue of the Greek Coins, Attica-Megaris-Aegina,* ed. R. S. Poole, The British Museum (London 1888).

BMC Lydia   B. V. Head *Catalogue of the Greek Coins of Lydia* The British Museum (London 1901).

Campbell   A. S. Campbell *Geology and History of Turkey* Petroleum Exploration Society, Libya (Tripoli 1971).

Cook   R. M. Cook *Greek Painted Pottery* (London 1960).

Demangel   R. Demangel *La frise ionique* (Paris 1932).

Dinsmoor   W. B. Dinsmoor *Architecture of Ancient Greece* (London 1950).

Greenewalt, "Exhibitionist"   C. H. Greenewalt, Jr. "An Exhibitionist from Sardis" in *Studies Presented to George M. A. Hanfmann,* eds. D. G. Mitten, J. G. Pedley, J. A. Scott (Cambridge, Mass./Mainz 1971) 29ff.

Hanfmann, *Letters*   G. M. A. Hanfmann *Letters from Sardis* (Cambridge, Mass. 1972).

Hanfmann-Waldbaum, "New Excavations"   G. M. A. Hanfmann and J. C. Waldbaum "New Excavations at Sardis and Some Problems of Western Anatolian Archaeology" in *Near Eastern Archaeology in the Twentieth Century: Essays in Honor of Nelson Glueck,* ed. J. A. Sanders (Garden City, N.Y. 1970) 307–326.

Hogarth, *Ephesus*   D. G. Hogarth *Excavations at Ephesus: The Archaic Artemisia* (London 1908).

Koch   H. Koch "Studien zu den campanischen Dachterrakotten," *RömMitt* 30 (1915) 1–115.

Larisa II   A. Åkerström and L. Kjellberg *Larisa II: Die architektonischen Terrakotten* (Stockholm 1940).

Munsell   Munsell Color Company, Inc., Baltimore, Md., soil color charts for color abbreviations and equivalents (1971).

Oleson   J. Oleson *Greek Numismatic Art: Coins of the Arthur Stone Dewing Collection* Fogg Art Museum, Harvard University (Cambridge, Mass. 1975).

Orlandos   A. K. Orlandos *Les matériaux de construction et la technique architecturale des anciens Grecs* Part 2 (Paris 1968).

Östenberg   C. E. Östenberg *Case Etrusche di Acquarossa* (Rome 1975).

Pedley   J. G. Pedley *Sardis in the Age of Croesus* (Norman, Okla, 1968).

Pryce   F. N. Pryce *Catalogue of Sculpture in the British Museum* I:1 (Oxford 1928).

Preusser   C. Preusser *Die Wohnhäuser in Assur,* *WVDOG* 64 (Berlin 1954).

Richter, *Handbook*[6]   G. M. A. Richter *A Handbook of Greek Art* 6th ed. rev. (New York/London 1969).

Richter, *Kouroi*   G. M. Richter *Kouroi: Archaic Greek Youths* (London 1960).

Richter, *Sculpture*   G. M. A. Richter *Sculpture and Sculptors of the Greeks* rev. ed. (New Haven 1950).

Robinson *Essays*   *Essays in Greek Coinage Presented to Stanley Robinson,* eds. C. N. Kraay and C. K. Jenkins (Oxford 1968).

Sardis I (1922)   H. C. Butler *Sardis* I, *The Excavations,* Part I: *1910–1914* (Leyden 1922).

Sardis II (1925)   H. C. Butler *Sardis* II, *Architecture,* Part I: *Temple of Artemis* (text and atlas of plates, Leyden 1925).

Sardis V (1924)   C. R. Morey *Sardis* V, *Roman and Christian Sculpture,* Part 1: *The Sarcophagus of Claudia Antonia Sabina* (Princeton 1924).

Sardis VI.1 (1916)   E. Littmann *Sardis* VI, *Lydian Inscriptions,* Part 1(Leyden 1916).

Sardis VI.2 (1924)   W. H. Buckler *Sardis* VI, *Lydian Inscriptions,* Part 2 (Leyden 1924).

Sardis VII (1932)   W. H. Buckler and D. M. Robinson *Sardis* VII, *Greek and Latin Inscriptions,* Part 1 (Leyden 1932).

Sardis X (1926)   T. L. Shear *Sardis* X, *Terra-cottas,* Part 1: *Architectural Terra-cottas* (Cambridge, U.K. 1926).

Sardis XI (1916)   H. W. Bell *Sardis* XI, *Coins,* Part 1: *1910–1914* (Leyden 1916).

Sardis XIII (1925)   C. D. Curtis *Sardis* XIII, *Jewelry and Gold Work,* Part 1: *1910–1914* (Rome 1925).

Sardis R1 (1975)   G. M. A. Hanfmann and J. C. Waldbaum *A Survey of Sardis and the Major Monuments outside the City Walls* Archaeological Exploration of Sardis Report 1 (Cambridge, Mass. 1975).

Sardis R2 (1978)   G. M. A. Hanfmann and N. H. Ramage *Sculpture from Sardis: The Finds through 1975* Archaeological Exploration of Sardis Report 2 (Cambridge, Mass. 1978).

Sardis M1 (1971)   G. E. Bates *Byzantine Coins* Archaeological Exploration of Sardis Monograph 1 (Cambridge, Mass. 1971).

Sardis M2 (1972)   J. G. Pedley *Ancient Literary Sources on Sardis* Archaeological Exploration of Sardis Monograph 2 (Cambridge, Mass. 1972).

Sardis M3 (1975)   R. Gusmani *Neue epichorische Schriftzeugnisse aus Sardis* (*1958–1971*) Archaeological Exploration of Sardis Monograph 3 (Cambridge, Mass. 1975).

Sardis M4 (1976)   C. Foss *Byzantine and Turkish Sardis* Archaeological Exploration of Sardis Monograph 4 (Cambridge, Mass. 1976).

Schweitzer   B. Schweitzer *Greek Geometric Art* (New York 1971).

Van Buren   E. D. Van Buren *Greek Fictile Revetments in the Archaic Period* (London 1926).

LYDIAN HOUSES
AND
ARCHITECTURAL
TERRACOTTAS

I LYDIAN DOMESTIC ARCHITECTURE

HISTORICAL INTRODUCTION

In material terms, the Lydians stand out as a distinct cultural group in the period from ca. 700 to 300 B.C. The Lydian people and their language probably existed as long ago as 2000 B.C. and continued into early Roman times, as happened with several different peoples in Anatolia. They came into prominence, however, in the seventh century; they seem to have slipped into the power vacuum caused by the collapse of the Phrygian Empire under the impact of repeated raids by the nomadic Kimmerians. Sardis itself was sacked too but recovery seems to have been swift and to have culminated in an unprecedented cultural flowering in the following century. Perhaps the Lydians were tributaries of the Phrygians, who became too weak to insist on their tribute. In this situation what would otherwise have gone in tribute could be applied to the growth and enrichment of the city. There must be a close connection between the change of dynasties in the city, from the Heraklids who had ruled since the time of the Trojan War to the Mermnads who would rule until the fateful end of Croesus, and the shaking of Phrygian power.

The daily life of the people of Sardis in the seventh and sixth centuries has not commanded attention equal to that accorded the political events and colorful scandals of the royal house of the Mermnad kings. This is natural enough, for until recently we were dependent on literary sources, which were much more concerned with the lives of people "of a certain status" and with pointing moral lessons than with describing the activities and preoccupations of ordinary folk. A conspectus of the historical and archaeological evidence can be found in Table 1.

Much, of course, can be gleaned by reading between the lines of the Greek and Roman sources, and the information gains in credibility insofar as it is introduced incidentally without reference to any didactic theme of the author. It is not the intention here to deny the interest or validity of the ancient writers for our subject. But a new tool exists in the form of the discoveries from sixteen years of excavation and study at Sardis by the Harvard-Cornell Expedition.[1] Excavation of the houses and shops of ordinary Lydian city-dwellers has laid bare their pots and pans and miscellaneous household goods, which throw much light on the way they lived.

Two sectors have produced major Lydian finds, Pactolus North (PN, Fig. 2 No. 10 and Fig. 3) and House of Bronzes-Lydian Trench (HoB, Fig. 2 No. 4 and Fig. 4). The former extends down to the banks of the Pactolus, within the valley; the latter is situated on the slopes of the foothills of the Acropolis just opposite the point where the Pactolus flows into the Hermus plain. Other sectors, sometimes mentioned, can be found on the plan: Pactolus Cliff (PC, Fig. 2 No. 13), still within the valley, Northeast Wadi (NEW

---

1. The current excavations by a Harvard-Cornell team were started in 1958 and preliminary reports have appeared annually (except 1969 season) in *BASOR* and *TürkArkDerg*. The final reports from seasons up to 1975 are in the course of preparation. So far two final reports and four monographs have appeared (see Bibliography under "Sardis"). A general overview of the excavations as they progressed can be found in G. M. A. Hanfmann, *Letters from Sardis* (Cambridge, Mass. 1972).

Table 1. Historical and archaeological chart.

—		Occasional polished celts of Neolithic type.
Early Bronze Age ca. 2500 B.C.		Settlements around the shore of the Gygaean Lake in the Hermus Valley.
Middle Bronze Age ca. 2000–1500		Lydians arrive? No material traces.
Late Bronze Age 1500–1300		Pithos cremation and circular hut remains found in HoB (Lydian Trench).
1300–1200		Imported Mycenaean pottery in Lydian Trench.
1200–1050 (Heraklid dynasty 1185)		House remains; Mycenaean and Protogeometric pottery in Lydian Trench.
Early Iron Age		Occupational debris; no house plans; connections both with Phrygian and Greek pottery. Wall fragments of uncertain date at PC.
ca. 680	Foundation of Mermnad dynasty by Gyges	Growth of the city? Relations with Assyrians and mainland Greeks.
Ca. 645	Kimmerian sack and death of Gyges	Burnt stratum in HoB and later a planned building complex in the area.
Ca. 610	Accession of Alyattes	Expansion to west.
561	Accession of Croesus	Expansion to east; confrontation with the Persian Empire. Gold refinery and Altar of Cybele in PN.
547	Capture of Sardis by Cyrus and death of Croesus	Burnt stratum in parts of PN.
499	Burning of Sardis by Ionians	Burnt stratum in parts of PN.
334	Sardis occupied by Alexander	Becomes nominally a Greek city.
Ca. 280	Building of Temple of Artemis	—
213	Capture of Sardis by Antiochus III of Syria	Uniform destruction level in PN.

Fig. 2 No. 16), and the Acropolis (Ac, Fig. 2 No. 20), the highest nearby area fit for both occupation and defense. Other areas, naturally, provide unstratified pieces, either just lying about or incorporated at random into later structures. Whatever its relevance, the actual findspot can be identified by reference to the overall grid, a series of 5-meter squares oriented roughly N/S according to the Roman Bath-Gymnasium complex (B, Fig. 2 No. 1), and originating at a point at the southeast corner of the main building. It can also be located vertically by reference to one of two datum points given the arbitrary level of 100. The first is found at the point mentioned above: the origin of the B grid. The other is on the stylobate of the Artemis Temple. The sectors PN, PC, and areas near the temple use the latter as the datum point. The House of Bronzes and areas near the Gymnasium use the former. In practice these anomalies are no great problem since the datum used is constant within a trench.[2]

2. For a full explanation of Sardis grids and levels see *Sardis* R1 (1975) 7—11.

What is more important is to get a general idea of where the chronological horizons are within each sector. For example in HoB:

Level no. 1   Late Roman mixed fill.
Level no. 2   Roman: water pipes and traceable ground surface.
Level no. 3   Hellenistic, ca. *100-99.
Level no. 4   Lydian level I, end of seventh century to early sixth century, ca. *99.00 (floors).
Level no. 5   Lydian level II, later seventh century, *98-97.5.
Level no. 6   Lydian level III, early to mid-seventh century, *97.5-96.5.
Level no. 7   Protogeometric, tenth or eleventh century, *94.75.
Level no. 8   Late Bronze Age (pithos burial, etc.) *91.

(Summarized from 1970 sector report by the late G. F. Swift, Jr.)

These chronological divisions are by no means absolute since at HoB there is a persistent slope to the ancient ground surfaces in a downwards direction, both from west to east and from south to north.

The levels at PN so far investigated show habitation from the late seventh century into the Hellenistic era (destruction of 213). A rough rule of thumb is that ca. *88.00 is Hellenistic and *86.00 is early sixth century.

The general history and overall extent of the Lydian culture at Sardis have been comprehensively set out in the first two chapters of *Sardis* R1 (1975). The growth of the Lydian Empire and the lives of its kings have been described by Pedley in *Sardis in the Age of Croesus*. We have not had, however, any attempt to describe the life of the general populace nor the physical conditions surrounding this life. In the absence of contemporary documentation the best evidence for day-to-day activity must be sought in the houses and the ordinary objects that have survived or left their mark in the earth.[3] We can draw some general conclusions about the way in which the Lydians were sheltered, and probably spent their days, from the houses we have excavated, which do not differ a great deal over several centuries and indeed share characteristics with the village houses of modern western Asia Minor

(Fig. 5). The series of buildings for which we have most evidence is dated from the seventh to the late third century B.C., but the overall design or construction methods do not change in any radical way. Thus, in my view, one may use some later features as hints for the interpretation of earlier obscurities.

Modern studies on housing in the Mediterranean world of this period are disappointing compared to those on more imposing monuments; this reflects to some extent the poor quality of the housing of the masses as well as the artistic and philosophical outlook of earlier generations of archaeologists. Without introducing any particular beliefs or dogma, I should merely like to explain how the physical circumstances of the life of ordinary Lydians can be recreated through our work and shown to be of great interest.

The material cultures of people bordering the Mediterranean had in the eighth and seventh centuries a broad similarity, reflecting in the main an equivalent stage of technological development, a similar response to climatic conditions, and in many cases similar geological surroundings. Obviously this generalization will not hold up under detailed analysis—one can see that the Greeks of Old Smyrna, which is by the sea, did not have the same kind of life as the Phrygians of Gordion, inland on a high plateau, or the Villanovans in Italy—but some activities and ways of doing things are common to many of these communities. This permits us to use analogies from the daily life of cultures at some distance from Lydia with confidence if the material or physical conditions are similar. The greatest outside influence in all matters was that of the Greeks, both of the mainland Greeks such as the Spartans or the Corinthians and of the Ionian Greeks such as Smyrniots, Samians, Rhodians, and Ephesians. This "borrowing" goes back to the beginnings of the Mermnad dynasty and the Lydian Empire and continues to its end: Gyges, the founder, sent gifts to the Oracle of Apollo at Delphi (Herodotus 1.13–14); Croesus, too, the last of the line, had dealings with Delphi and Sparta (Herodotus 1.70) and financed the rebuilding of the Artemisium at Ephesus (Herodotus 1.92). One may also assume some dealings with the Carians (from Carian inscriptions found in Sardis), and the Phrygians (from decorated pottery patterns and the highly polished blackware which is common at Gordion in early levels and occurs most frequently at Sardis among early seventh century material). If we wish to search further afield we need only remember that Gyges had diplomatic relations with the Assyrian kings (*Sardis* M2 [1972] 292–295, comment and further references) and that there was a very ancient pattern of trade between Anatolia and Mesopotamia.

---

3. The Lydian pottery will be presented *in extenso* by C. H. Greenewalt, Jr., and small finds by R. S. Thomas in forthcoming volumes in the Sardis series. For preliminary reports on the pottery see Greenewalt, *California Studies in Classical Antiquity* 1 (1968) 139–154; 3 (1970) 55–89; 5 (1972) 113–145; 6 (1973) 91–122. Assemblages of pots from a ritual meal, idem, "Ritual Dinners in Early Historic Sardis," University of California Press, forthcoming.

An especially interesting and delightful aspect of Lydian architecture is the extensive use of decorated terracotta tiles, which served both as protection against rain and as ornament. They are used on the roof itself and on the eaves and the gable ends. Friezes are put together consisting of floral and patterned chains and scenes with human and animal figures. These friezes are not only modeled in relief but also painted in fired earth colors to accentuate the pattern. We find this kind of decoration all over the world of Greek influence in the Archaic era, but it was particularly popular among the cities of Asia Minor and the area influenced by them. The recent excavations have given Sardis by far the most varied collection of these pieces yet found and this study will present them, after describing the construction and layout of the houses they decorated.

STRUCTURE

House Walls

Lydian domestic architecture is based upon building with mud brick; even the Palace of Croesus was built of it (Vitruvius 2.8.9–10; Pliny *NH* 35.172). The buildings were made either of individual bricks of sun baked clay or of larger sections of earth rammed into a frame set on the wall (pisé, described in detail below). The Lydians handled the material in a different way from that used by their neighbors and predecessors, the Phrygians and the Hittites, for there is no evidence for the use of structural timber in any of the buildings yet discovered at Sardis. This may be explained by the fact that the largest wall designed to carry a mud brick superstructure found at Sardis is 0.90 m. in width, and many of the walls at Gordion and at Hattusas, where there is extensive use of timber framing, are several meters thick.

In 1977 a monumental mudbrick structure which does make use of timber was discovered but it does not alter the general thrust of the argument. This is because the structure, which has not been fully excavated, is likely to have been part of the city wall and not a residential structure. There were, for instance, layers of horizontal timbers at ca. 0.70 m. intervals but no vertical pieces.

The description of the "Burned Phrygian Building" at Gordion, whose overall dimensions are very large, is utterly unlike any traces yet found at Sardis.

It was built of crude brick strengthened by a framework of vertical wooden posts and horizontal wooden beams in both faces of the walls tied together at intervals by cross-ties running through the thickness. In general the walls are preserved to a height of about 1 m. above the floor or to the level of the first horizontal beam set in their faces. They are divided into alternating "piers," roughly square, and "niches," oblong recesses where the vertical posts have burned out. Each niche seems to have contained not a single post but a pair of wooden verticals filled between with broken brick. The posts or verticals did not extend to the full height of the wall, as might have been expected: instead they ran only to the level of the horizontal beams.

The second layer of brickwork, between the first and second horizontal beams (probably nine courses of bricks) had its own series of wooden verticals, placed above the piers of the lower layer. [R. S. Young, *AJA* 61 (1957) 321]

In addition, one finds wood used in the narrower walls at the above-mentioned sites so that we are obviously dealing with different traditions. Could it be that the architectural tradition at Sardis is more directly connected to that of Mesopotamia than to the central Anatolian plateau? Building traditions in both domestic and palatial architecture of the late Assyrian period would seem to bear this out. Indeed, the absence of wood for structural elements in the walls in the houses at Assur is specifically contrasted to its use at Zincirli (Preusser, 17), which is in the Hittite tradition.

The house walls at Sardis are composed of a socle of fieldstones with a superstructure of mud brick. This socle is laid directly onto the ground; trenching to set foundations below the ground level has not been distinguished. The original floor in most buildings is about 10 cm. above the bottom of the wall. The bases of the walls are rarely wider than the upper portions and it is unusual to find much larger stones in any but the lowest course; thus no great concern for stability even in appearance is exhibited. The stones are set in mud mortar and laid in courses. The thinner walls are normally two stones wide, the thicker often have a rubble core. The rubble varies from the faces only in that the elements are rather smaller and thus distinct. There is no sign of loose filling and there are no cases of headers through the wall to bind the faces together (Fig. 6).

Most walls are of medium sized field or river stones (0.20 to 0.25 m. long). These are usually of grayish schist or gneiss, which is the basic rock of the nearby Tmolus range; less often and normally in inferior and later walls one finds quartz lumps. Pieces of the friable local sandstone, both purple and yellow, are found frequently in the excavations near the Pactolus, but the natural rock itself is found in bands on the slopes of the Acropolis and Necropolis, where many of the chamber tombs are cut. It is not impossible that the quarrying of these tombs provided some of the material for our walls; certainly it would have had to be cut and brought in, since it is not hard enough to survive rolling in the riverbed or the action of water for any length of time.

Some outside corners are distinctly rounded, especially in HoB, but better built structures from the mid-sixth century on have carefully squared corners, many with intentional alternation of long and short sides of the stone (Fig. 7). Indeed it seems that the corners may very well have been built first, to ensure a fit and to make sure that the walls would be plumb. There is a distinct triangular area of better fitted stones at the corners of the buildings, where flat schist pieces are used, while the areas between are much more haphazard. It is not unusual in bricklaying to build up the corners first even nowadays; a particularly persuasive analogy comes from the early stages of a modern house in a mountain valley of the Tmolus range to the southeast of Sardis (Fig. 8). Some of the schist pieces in the walls are more worked than is evident at first, but one must also note the natural suitability of the material for wall building. Its flat cleavage planes lend themselves readily to the making of pieces with parallel faces without much effort. It is still favored today as a material for foundations and carted in from some distance. The most notable examples of its careful use are all in PN—especially the altar, units 1 and 2, and the apsidal buildings (see plan Fig. 3). This technique of using flat regular stones was at one time taken to be a mark of the Persian period (*BASOR* 162, 26, 29, fig. 14), but is now viewed as typical of the late period of the Lydian Empire. It is unlikely even that the coming of the Persians had any great effect upon house building.

There are two structures in PN which have small limestone chips added as packing between the stones. Some of these chips had flat worked edges, which suggests that there may have been ashlar buildings or monuments nearby; this is further suggested by the later reuse of large limestone blocks which had been roughly cut and inscribed by the Lydians.

Ashlar masonry is unknown as yet in domestic buildings. The ashlar masonry of the walls discovered on the north face of the Acropolis (*BASOR* 162, 37f.; 206, 16f., figs. 5–7) is of course very fine and might belong to a palace or public building. Evidence against this as a hint of fine domestic buildings as yet undiscovered are the statements of Vitruvius and Pliny, mentioned above, that the palace of Croesus was of mud brick. This is not to propose that the palace of Croesus was crudely finished on the exterior, for we must certainly imagine fine stone facing if not a solid

ashlar wall as foundation, and some protection and embellishment for the doorjambs.[4]

Besides the sharp-sided pieces and flat-faced walls, we find use of much smaller, rounded pieces of schist laid flat one upon the other to form decorative patterns. This is not done throughout the wall for it would be very weak but is found at corners or at wall ends for doorjambs (Fig. 9). On occasion, courses are laid in which stones of the same course overlap so that an oblique effect is gained on the face. Sometimes the next course overlaps in the reverse direction to produce a herringbone effect (Fig. 10), but this is not carried up throughout the wall; in one place only does it certainly recur higher up—a kind of decorative coursing.

An additional inference which may be drawn from this delight in the stones themselves is that the walls of this era were not all covered with mud plaster as is commonly supposed, but some stood bare and open to view. To support this opinion is the fact that in only one place have we found mud plaster *in situ* (HoB unit L, Fig. 11); elsewhere no traces have been recorded.

The use of both mud brick and pisé, mentioned above, is confirmed from discoveries of each *in situ* at different points, although in other places it was impossible to differentiate the two. The bricks frequently have a good deal of straw temper or binding material, which is especially noticeable in burnt bricks from the furnaces in Pactolus North, where the imprints are obvious, although the actual stalks have burned away. By contrast there is no sign of it in the pisé. As I use the term, mud brick refers to unbaked, discrete pieces of clayey earth shaped in a wooden frame to a standard size and laid in mud mortar much as a modern fired brick or concrete block is laid in cement or lime mortar. The technique of pisé requires the making of a form of planks as thick as the wall (about 1.50 m. long, 0.60 m. high). This box-like construction is filled with layers of damp clayey earth which are compacted with poles to make a piece of wall very much like those produced today in poured concrete. The beauty of pisé really lies in its strength, which is said to be greater than that of laid mud brick. The best surviving example of the use of pisé is the west wall in unit 28 of PN (see plan, Fig. 3), which is ca. 0.40 m. wide, corresponding very closely to the modern width for pisé walls (Fig. 12).

The most common dimensions for individual bricks are 0.40 by 0.25 by 0.08–0.10 m., a proportion which is

4. On the evidence for the palace of Croesus see now G. M. A. Hanfmann, "On the Palace of Croesus," *Festschrift für Frank Brommer*, ed. U. Höckmann and A. Krug (Mainz 1977) 145–154, pl. 41.

approximately equivalent to 4:3:1. This size is found in HoB and PN particularly, where by far the most Lydian remains have been excavated. So far no bricks have been found which correspond exactly to Vitruvius' proportions for "the bricks which are called 'Lydian' in Greek" (2.3.3; i.e. one and a half feet long and one foot wide), although some of a different kind he describes, the *Pentadora,* might be represented by the square bricks in HoB (building K) which are 0.40 by 0.40 m. In 1977 a monumental mud brick structure of the seventh century B.C. was discovered, over 6 m. high and at least 12 m. wide. It is unknown at present what its function was: either we have unearthed a small section of the city wall or a part of an imposing platform. The average size of the bricks from the sounding was 0.50 by 0.30 by 0.10–0.12 which comes close to the proportions Vitruvius gives for the "Lydian" brick if he is using as his unit the Doric foot of 0.327 m.

By comparing what seem to be standard sizes in Lydian buildings one may see that the Lydians used a foot approximating the Ionic foot of 0.295 to 0.296 m. Thus, frequent widths for the stone socle of mud brick walls are 0.30, 0.45, and 0.60 m., and 0.90 m. is likely for door openings. All these dimensions are multiples of the basic unit. This is borne out to a considerable extent by the dimensions of the chamber tombs at the royal cemetery of Bin Tepe, which are in general made of very finely cut and carefully fitted masonry. It is likely that extreme fidelity to a whole number of units is not to be expected since most of the corners are not quite square. In that case the final fitting must have taken precedence over the projected dimensions. It is, however, notable that in the tomb chambers there is a very large proportion of lengths of about 2.00 m. If we take the range between 2.10 and 1.90 m. for confirmed dimensions of chambers, we find that out of a total of thirty-five measurements from chamber tombs dug or examined during the Harvard-Cornell excavations and the dimensions given by Choisy (*RA* 32 [1876] 73–81), eleven fall within it and the average length is 2.015; and in the largest number of instances the single length measures 2.00 m. The closest multiples of 0.295 to these figures are 1.991 m. and 2.065 m. ($6^3/_4$ and 7 feet respectively), which is suggestive but not conclusive.

The standard brick size of 0.40 by 0.25 by 0.08 (mentioned above) and the pisé thickness, do not at first sight seem consonant with the unit of 0.295, but on examination it will be seen that if divisions of sixths are taken into account (which is normal for currency division), approximate values of $1^1/_3$, $^5/_6$, and $^1/_3$ are obtained, giving a ratio of 8:5:2. R. Ross Holloway has suggested to me that the ancient Lydian foot was 0.32 m. in length and divided into 16 dactyls. This would make the bricks $1^1/_4$ by $^3/_4$ by $^1/_4$ and the walls a little short of 1 ft., $1^1/_2$ ft., or 2 ft., a discrepancy caused by working within two string lines. I am happy to accept the suggestion that the Lydian foot may have been divided into 16, but I see no reason why the smaller unit should correspond to a whole number of metric units, which are, after all, modern constructs.

Not enough substantial brick walls have been found at Sardis to pick out favorite methods of bonding and building in brick. We can see from HoB building H (discussed below) that the Lydians were capable of using irregular sizes and half bricks when it suited them, but we have not been able to analyse their methods of laying bricks on walls whose width does not correspond to an even number of the principal dimensions of their bricks. At least, however, the difficulty occasioned by the size 0.36 by 0.27 by 0.09 m., which was once thought to be the standard Lydian size (*BASOR* 182, 12), can now be obviated since by the judicious use of half-bricks walls can be built which correspond very well to the most common sizes for the stone socles, which are 0.30, 0.45, and 0.60. There is no uniform height at which the mud brick was begun: some stone walls stand bare to a height of 1.80 m., whereas others have mud brick applied after one or two courses only.

Design and Interiors

So far as one can tell, most Lydian houses were "single cell" buildings of a very simple type. That is to say that the main structure was built to a plan which would form one large room, very much like village houses in the same area both today and in the past (Fig. 13). Having a shape of this kind still allows many interior arrangements, as the sketch of the late eighteenth century A.D. house in Tobermory in the west of Scotland shows (Fig. 14). It does not require that there be only one room. Most of the methods of secondary division within the house depend upon the use of wooden timbers set in the wall, presumably for the attachment of room dividers slighter than the main walls. In the absence of any particular traces other than slots in the walls we have concluded that these dividers were made of organic materials: either a more or less permanent arrangement of light wattle and daub or a curtain with the texture of a rug, which could be drawn across the room at will. A problem here, which cannot be ignored, is that, except in one early seventh century building (at HoB W0-5/S95-103 *97.4 floor), there is no record of post holes, and so the possibility of only a partial division (by means of a wall coming a little way into the room) seems out of the question. Another problem which must be faced is the relation of the divider to the ceiling or roof. There is no difficulty in attaching the curtain or even a light wall to the crossbeams, but if the roof is pitched rather than flat a gap is created.

Openings for doors frequently seem to be about 0.60 or 0.90 m. but, in the absence of clear threshold stones (or traces), it is not possible to be sure that these dimensions represent a traditional size. This would correspond to about two or three Lydian feet respectively. It is not even certain, though very probable, that the door openings were faced with a wooden surround. A limestone house model from Samos shows distinct traces of recessed jambs (cf.) Schweitzer, fig. 239). At PN particularly the ends of walls for door openings were often carefully squared off, but even where several courses of wall remain there are no traces of holes where jambs might have been attached. It is not necessary, but likely, that the openings had actual wooden doors, but we have not found any provision for pivoting doors. Interior openings may very well have been closed by curtains. There is only one clear instance of a window (PN unit 1, north wall W280/S337, plan Fig. 3 and Fig. 22), but the late G. F. Swift, Jr., the excavator at HoB, concluded that there had been several windows on the south side of HoB building L, a structure of the middle to late seventh century. In any event we may certainly suppose that random holes were punched in the walls (as happens sometimes today). In the example at PN, according to the excavator, an original door was converted into the window, which may explain why the supports are so wide, ca. 1.50 m., when modern windows, especially those made by casual holes, are only about 0.45 m. wide.

HoB Building H

Several houses have individual interior features but they are almost all found together in building H in the Lydian Trench of Sector HoB (Fig. 15). This house, which we interpret as belonging to a craftsman, might form, so to speak, a model house. It measures 8.0 by 3.2 m., bigger than most but still close to its fellows. Near the southwest corner is a small, almost square foundation of small stones (1.0 m. by 0.75 m. by 0.30 m.) which is divided into two roughly equal compartments. It has been suggested that they are supports for a wooden cupboard or chest. They could, however, be storage containers in themselves, either for loose material or smaller containers such as jars or boxes; it is unlikely that they were hearths or ovens, since no ash or charcoal was observed and the mud mortar showed no signs of reddening by fire. Indeed, there was a distinct hearth or small furnace in two compartments

made of clay and burnt red and hard, just beside this structure on the south side. Beside that in turn, attached to the west wall, was a bench-like structure ca. 2.0 m. by 0.5 m. made of stones raised a little above the floor (0.15 m. to 0.20 m.). There was a narrow slit in the enclosure wall at W35.5/S120.5 which was too thin for access (it may not have gone all the way through) and was therefore regarded as provision for a timber inserted to attach wooden fittings. At the south end of H in its north-south walls were two matching vertical grooves, 1.25 and 1.50 m. from the south wall. The line between them is more or less parallel with the south wall, which has a gentle bulge outwards. The resulting space seems rather cramped for most activities but is a possible working area for someone squatting on his haunches at the low clay and stone platform against the south wall. Another possibility is that the bench is a later addition and the partition planned for the first phase of the house is no longer in use. This arrangement would give much more room.

The door in this house was on the long side (northeast corner) and was 0.60 m. wide; the condition of the wall ends was too poor to make any definite inferences about the door fittings. It is probable that there was a window in the north end, since there was a mass of mud bricks in the center of the wall which did not show a uniform pattern of bricklaying (Fig. 16). This suggested a repair or alteration, and the immediate reason for it which comes to mind is the presence of a window in the original layout. I know of a window in the short, north wall of a house in the sector near the Pactolus and can imagine others in buildings where the walls are not sufficiently preserved for us to tell. In fact, judging from present-day practices, one could supply windows in any part of the walls where it was structurally practicable.

Since no tiles were found in the debris or nearby, it is logical to infer that the building had a pitched and thatched roof or a flat, earth roof such as is still found in the village of Sart Mustafa and many places in the vicinity (Figs. 5, 17). I have not seen in modern Turkey a steep, thatched roof of the kind that one finds in Holland or in Britain, but there is no reason to rule the method out for that reason. Herodotus (5.101) mentions roofs made of reeds but he refers to the tall, heavy kind—perhaps bullrushes, or the variety *Arundo donax*, which grows to a height of 4 to 5 m.[5]—

5. "A tall bamboo-like reed with tough woody leafy stems thicker than a finger . . . stems 4–5 m. high . . . Probably originated in the Orient, but it has long been cultivated in the Mediterranean region where it is fully naturalized. Widely used for basket-making, walking sticks, fishing rods, and for making windbreaks and shelters. It is the largest grass in Europe" (Oleg Polunin and Anthony Huxley, *Flowers of the Mediterranean* [London 1967] 199).

rather than the shorter grassy variety commonly used as thatch in northern Europe. This means that in practical terms it is quite as possible to match his description with flat as with pitched roofs because the longer, more woody variety of reed is commonly used in modern mud brick houses or outbuildings. It is also possible to imagine that by the late sixth century the practice of covering roofs with terracotta tiles would have become quite common. This suggestion is supported by evidence from the excavations near the Pactolus, but the tiles are by no means so common as to require their universal or even frequent use.

The excavations have produced no evidence for free-standing furniture in the houses. In building H there was no built-in sleeping platform and we should imagine the owner and his family resting on wooden beds like the stone examples found in several tombs. They would probably be collapsible, rather like some camp beds or cots today, fit to be put away in the daytime.

Blankets or quilts could be stored in the built-in cupboards or in special chests. Many examples might be cited from classical literature, such as the chest of Cypselus, the chest which served Danaë and the infant Perseus as a boat, and the frequent references to chests full of linen or woolens in the *Odyssey* (2.339; 8.438; 13.10).

A chair or a stool might complete the domestic furniture. Judging by today's practices in comparable situations, squatting on the haunches and eating at ground level would have been usual; reclining at tables was reserved for the aristocracy. We may see this in the terracotta friezes from Larisa (frieze VII, *Larisa* II 64–80, pls. 22–33), scenes on Corinthian and Attic vases, and in Etruscan tomb paintings, and we know it continued for a very long time in the Greco-Roman world.

The kitchen and dining equipment for a Lydian family would consist of several types of jars for storage of different liquids and dry goods. Jugs of different sizes would be used to serve these liquids and the dry goods could go onto plates or into bowls. If the storage vessels (pithoi), for example, contained grain, that might be ground on the family quern to make it into flour which in turn would be baked into bread. Very probably this would be done on the flat, coarse clay rectangle that is even now known as a "bread tray" (Fig. 18).

"The House of the Priest" (PN unit 28)

Unit 28 at PN (Fig. 19) merits extensive description because it is especially large and because it is retangular and shows dividing walls. This unit, the so-called

House of the Priest, is a long building in the area W255-263/S337-351 (Figs. 3, 19, foreground). It is 13.5 by 5.0 m. externally. The exterior walls, of which only the west and part of the south end remain, are about 0.40 m. thick; the plan of the building was revealed by robber trenches filled with that same gravel which overlay a secondary floor. Part of the south end of the west wall still retains about 0.60 m. of mud brick covering. There were no signs of the use of individual bricks as have been found elsewhere (for example HoB, H and K and PN furnaces).

At the upper level the building had two rooms; to the north 3.4 by 4.0 m., to the south 9.2 by 4.0 m. At a lower level, which had a floor about 0.60 below the upper floor, the building had three rooms: the north 3.4 by 4.0 m., the middle 3.3 by 4.0 m., the south 5.4 by 4.0 m. The wall between the middle and south rooms had not been robbed, presumably because it was covered by the later floor. In its center was a rectangular dip filled with clay which measured 0.90 m. across (Fig. 20). This must be interpreted as a doorway.

There is no way of telling where the main door of the building was situated. The west wall is more or less intact with no obvious openings; it is less well preserved beyond the robbed crosswall and this may have afforded a door to the west. On the other hand it is quite possible that there was a door near the southeast corner. This supposition was made even more likely by the discovery in 1970 of an oblique wall and cobbled pavement butting against the line of the robbed north-south wall in the area W259/S349. The other outside walls are robbed and the north wall is obscured under a substantial later structure incorporating a large water channel.

The structure was clearly a house (whatever extra functions it may have served connected with the Altar of Cybele just to the west—hence its popular name, "the House of the Priest"), and the only object found within the structure which was not obviously domestic was a small bronze hawk's head (M68.1:7597; *BASOR* 199, 18, fig. 11), which was filled with lead and may have found secondary use as a weight; there is certainly no provision for attaching it to a handle. The pottery finds indicate a date before the middle of the sixth century for the original building; the final phase of the upper floor must be contemporary with the inundation of most of the area and the resulting thick gravel deposit.

This unit is notable for its size and regular plan, resembling more the separate structures found in the HoB area than most of the units at PN, which frequently have party walls or are very close together. An important exception to this is found about 10 m. to the west in unit 30, which measures about 9.3 by 4.8 m. on the outside and has no interior divisions.

PN Units 1, 2, and 3

Units 1 and 2 form one of the best preserved and most complex structures in PN (Figs. 3, 21). They were once interpreted as wholly domestic buildings whose floors were colored red as the result of destruction by fire: industry was expressly ruled out. Discoveries in 1968 and 1969, however, showed that the area was used for gold refining during the early part of the sixth century and that at least part of the structure was intimately associated with a series of furnaces built against the west wall of unit 2, which was partially robbed later. These furnaces and associated processes for the refining of gold produced the reddened mud brick as typical debris. At a later time these units were converted to domestic use.

The first configuration of the two units was much like the smaller version indicated by dotted lines on the plan (Fig. 3) with the north-south walls slightly to the east. It is unclear whether the shape was exactly the same but the dimensions of unit 1 were at least 2.6 by 3.2 m. and perhaps as much as 2.6 by 9.0 m. Unit 2 would then be 2.6 by 5.0 m. or else absorbed into the single unit with 1.

The second stage was distinctly two rooms (3.4 by 2.8 m. and 5.1 by 3.8 m.) with well-built walls (ca. 0.60 m. thick) which are preserved to a height of 1.40 m. at the northeast corner of unit 1. At the northeast corners, particularly, much larger stones are used for the bottom courses as if the east wall were of special importance. There was a door in the east wall of unit 1, 0.90 m. wide, whose jambs were carefully finished; there was also a door at this time in the north wall which was later converted into a window by closing the space with a thin, curving screen wall (Fig. 22, right). The general level of the original threshold was raised, too, so as to form a bench or window seat. The width of the gap in the wall was ca. 1.50 m. according to our plan. In unit 2 there was a door in the east wall at the southeast corner whose jambs were not well finished and it may well have been knocked out of the wall rather than planned in the design of the original house.

In the third stage of this complex, the west wall was moved further west and the dividing wall perhaps no longer used, thus making an irregular rectangle whose maximum dimensions are 9.0 m. and 5.0 m. Unit 3 was probably an open area both in its industrial phase and later.

Units 1, 2, and 3 seem to make a complex of a two-roomed house and yard with a small shed-like addition to the north (see Fig. 23). The original floor of the mid-sixth century seems to have been at *86.35 and there was a still higher floor at ca. *86.55 which was finally abandoned some time in the fifth century. Since there is at present no evidence for the dating of the upper floors, one must rely upon the fact that the whole area was covered by a deep gravel deposit, but one cannot be sure when. One might speculate that it was some way into the Persian Era since the altar, which was practically buried in the same gravel, was built up solid with regularly sized stones and chips, in quite a different way from that used by the Lydians. One might suppose that it would then be suitable for Persian ritual and, indeed, has been referred to as a Fire Altar rather than an Altar of Cybele.

Roofs and Tiles

The evidence we have at Sardis and in Lydia generally for the roofing systems of ancient houses is spread over a long span of time. The earliest traces we have are from HoB (Fig. 24) and consist of scorched lumps of clay/mud which have preserved the imprints of reeds or thin twigs; these are thought to have come from a wattle and daub roof (*BASOR* 170, 7, fig. 5) dating from early in the Late Bronze Age. Traces of a lightly thatched roof dating from the early seventh century B.C. were found in the same area but the surrounding structure was insubstantial (*BASOR* 186, 33, fig. 5). The thatch was made of thin reeds or straw, which had remained in a carbonized state beneath the earth. From later in the seventh century comes additional evidence for thatching with reeds, in the form of a piece of clay (accidentally fired in a burning) which preserves impressions on both its upper and lower surfaces (Figs. 25, 26). The different forms mirrored on the two faces indicate that the practice was to place poles close together horizontally, to lay clayey mud over them, and to put reeds vertically on the top surface of the mud. This combination would seal the roof and convey the rain water towards the ground.

The only evidence other than these examples consists of fragments of baked clay roof tiles and decorative architectural terracottas. There are fragments of architectural terracottas from contexts which are dated in the late seventh century but they are not so common as to indicate universal use on every class of roofed structure. Given the virtual indestructibility of baked clay, we must conclude that their rarity now corresponds to a certain rarity then; we can say, also, that there is a higher incidence of ceramic roof tiles in the later Lydian levels than in the early ones.

It seems very probable that there were always some houses (of the meanest kind) that were not roofed with baked clay tiles. There are whole villages in Anatolia today (especially in the east) where tiles are not found, and the shanty towns surrounding large cities in many Mediterranean lands are built of an enormous variety of materials for walls and for roofs. In the absence of specific evidence I have assumed, following Herodotus (5.101), that most houses had thatched roofs.

[The Ionians] were prevented from sacking the place after its capture by the fact that most of the houses in Sardis were constructed of reeds, reed thatch being used even on the few houses which were built of brick. One house was set alight by a soldier, and the flames rapidly spread until the whole town was ablaze. The outlying parts were all burning, so the native Lydians and such Persians as were staying there, caught in a ring of fire and unable to get clear of the town, poured into the market square on either bank of the Pactolus, where they were forced to stand on their defence. [Aubrey de Selincourt, trans.]

I would include in the category of thatched roofs any kind of interlacing of twigs or grasses and the parallel placing of bundles of reeds. This would include also the flat earth roofs mentioned earlier. The use of architectural terracottas does not, of itself, mean that a roof must have been pitched and tiled; the angled terracottas common at Gordion (cf. *ATK*, fig. 41) were fixed to the walls, at the eaves or even lower, as were flat decorative plaques, but not necessarily as part of a system of guttering for which other combinations of tiles—with spouts—were used. A suitable place can be seen in Figure 27, which shows a mud brick house in the older style, from the village of Sart Mustafa, which has a narrow frieze of baked bricks just below the eaves.

II THE TERRACOTTAS

with a contribution by Diana C. Kamilli

INTRODUCTION

The use of fired clay pieces as decorative cladding was a feature of Lydian architecture, as it was of much Greek architecture, too, in the late seventh and sixth centuries B.C. The petrographic examination of the clay bodies of a sample of the excavated pieces confirms the localization of their manufacture at Sardis. Both visual comparison of the texture and the lack of chaff in the manufacture relates the terracottas to the commonest Lydian ceramics of the same era at Sardis and indicates that they were locally made. This does not by any means rule out the thesis of strong Ionian influence and an ultimate origin at Corinth,[1] but the lack of any examples of terracottas with figurative motifs making a frieze on the mainland of Greece makes it difficult to assign that specific invention to Corinth. Terracottas from Corinth and from places directly influenced by her are normally composed of flat surfaces enlivened by the painting of patterns from decorative architectural moldings. So for this special class of terracottas one might find an origin in Ionia[2] or even further east, while still allowing to Corinth the original popularization of clay roof tiles and the creation of large-scale sculpture in terracotta. In view of the intermingling of invention and refinement we must think in terms of a trade in designs or even in molds from which our terracottas might have been made. The extraordinary resemblance between star and scroll simas from Sardis and Gordion gives a strong hint of this. Another possibility, often mentioned in connection with different crafts, is the employment of itinerant masters who came from other centers, leaving their stamp upon the work even while creating in an alien mode (*ATK*, 202). As it is, we must be alert to notice the local features of the designs, while at the same time seeing that they are true to the overall concepts of archaic Greek art in western Asia Minor.

The tiles were made by pressing sheets of soft clay into a form. Joins can often be seen at the corners, and the uneven layering to be seen in the broken sections (**6** Figs. 28a-b) shows that additions of clay were frequently made to build up the thickness. This will be further dealt with in individual catalogue entries, especially **1**. There are no bumpy finger marks on the inside or backs of the tiles; usually however there are many close parallel lines to be seen on the surface (Fig. 29 back of **27**). These lines are in most cases the result of the finishing technique to remove the excess thickness of clay. Some lines must come from nicks in the blade but most come from picking up small pieces of grit which were used for tempering the clay.

We do not know what the forms themselves were made of; both plaster and terracotta have been suggested and wood is a possibility too. In the absence of indications we must depend on comparisons with contemporary practice in other places, since actual examples of molds made of fired clay are recorded from central Italy in considerable numbers (Andrén, cxvif. with footnotes and references) and one or two have been found in peninsular Greece (Van Buren, 19, 55). It is possible that there was a form for the upper sur-

---

1. Pliny *NH* 35.151–152, on the inventions of Butades, a potter; *ATK*, 204, 257f.
2. Cf. Demangel, 133ff. and Van Buren, xvii.

face and backs of sima tiles which was applied to the upper surface and would squeeze out the bumps and help produce a uniform thickness. The removal of the completed tiles would have been simple after drying because of the related shrinkage—as much as 13% in some clay bodies depending upon the amount of temper, ca. 5 to 6% in clay obtained from Urganlı, not far from Sardis, which fires very like the ancient material.[3] Even with the lower figure, as long as the change is sufficient to break the bond between the surface of the mold and the tile, removal should not be difficult. There is no doubt that the reliefs were retouched with a sharp instrument after being removed from the mold, since it is impossible to get some of the sharp edges required without using a process of clay casting with liquid slip, which was certainly not in general use at this time, as observation of broken pieces indicates. At this stage, too, the paint was applied—before the clay body became too dry for the colored slip to bond to it satisfactorily. Of course one can deal with this problem by dampening the surface with a sponge or a rag, but it is risky.

The range of colors is small, consisting of the usual four, familiar from Archaic Greek pottery: black, white, red, and brown. The names may be the same but the actual shades are rather different. An approximate general description and an evaluation according to the Munsell code (see bibliography) taken in bright daylight is:

Black	Opaque Black	N.25/0
White	Creamy White	10YR8/2
Red	Orangy Red	2.5YR5/8
Brown	Dark Matte	2.5YR2.5/2

The colors are generally matte except for the orangy red, which has a considerable sheen. This bright color is most noticeable on the sima tiles and frieze plaques. As far as one can tell, the faces of the antefixes were not painted unless there was a thin "wash" covering them which has not survived.

Mineral Analysis of the Clay Bodies
by Diana C. Kamilli

The results of petrographic thin section mineral analysis of ten architectural terracotta fragments are shown in Table 2. The samples chosen appear in hand

sample to be relatively uniform in color and grain size. The paste is fine grained and coarse temper is rare. In thin section, some show the orientation of mica flakes characteristic of clay pressed into mold forms; this feature, however, is also dependent on the relative percentage of mica to equigranular minerals and its absence is not significant.

The mineral assemblage typical of ceramics from Sardis is shown at the end of Table 2 and was compiled from analyses of over 100 sherds of the archaic through the late Byzantine periods.[4] Such sherds are assumed to represent local manufacture both because this assemblage commonly occurs at the site and because analysis of local rocks shows that all materials found in these ceramics may be present in the immediate vicinity. Sardis is located in the western part of Turkey near Izmir and the Gediz River. The local rocks are composed mostly of folded, low to intermediate grade metamorphic schist, marble, and gneiss of either PreCambrian or Paleozoic age.[5] Petrographic analysis shows that the schists contain quartz, untwinned feldspar (orthoclase in part), Na plagioclase, biotite, and muscovite. Overlying the metamorphic rocks are several layers of unmetamorphosed sandstone, conglomerate, and arkose, probably Mesozoic in age. These contain derivatives of the schist, but in places also microcline, epidote, and traces of chert. The schists and marbles of Sardis belong to one of the intermediate crystalline massifs of Western Turkey, but the site is in a zone transitional to the intermediate fold system mentioned by Ilhan in Campbell, 159. All of Turkey is part of the Mediterranean sector of the Alpine orogenic belt.

As shown in Table 2, the mineral assemblage of all ten Lydian architectural terracotta samples strongly resembles that of the standard Sardis ceramic mineralogy and is characterized by the presence of quartz, untwinned feldspar, traces of Na plagioclase, biotite, muscovite, hematite (both as grains and staining), and varying amounts of chert. Several samples also contain traces of microcline, chlorite, magnetite, epidote, and schist fragments. No sample has Ca plagioclase, primary calcite (although some samples contain traces

3. High shrinkage data from R. H. Johnston, "Pottery Practices During the 6th–8th Centuries B.C. at Gordion in Central Anatolia" (Diss. Pennsylvania State University 1970) 56, fig. 5, p. 62, table V; low shrinkage data from verbal communication with E. Hostetter, in the course of experiments in the field at Sardis, 1976.

4. The results of analyses are to be published in the Sardis series with each group of ceramics. A preliminary presentation of results is in J. A. Scott and D. C. Kamilli, "Late Byzantine Glazed Pottery from Sardis," *XVᵉ Congrès international d'études byzantines* (Athens, forthcoming).

5. Geologic Map of Turkey: Izmir Sheet, Mineral Research and Exploration Institute of Turkey (Ankara 1962); *Sardis* I (1922) Appendix I; R. Brinkmann, "The Geology of Western Anatolia" in Campbell, 171–190; E. Ilhan, "The Structural Features of Turkey" in Campbell, 159–170.

Table 2. Sherd mineralogy of mold-made Lydian architectural terracottas and contemporary wheel-made lamps. The "typical Sardian ceramic assemblage" represents a summary of data from over 100 sherds of all types and ages from the site. "Untwinned feldspar" includes both orthoclase and untwinned Na plagioclase. "Secondary calcite" is calcite that fills holes and cracks in the sherd, and therefore must have precipitated post-firing. "Tr" = trace.

Sample	Catalogue or inventory no.	Estimated % coarse mineral fraction	Quartz	Untwinned feldspar	Na plagioclase	Ca plagioclase	Microcline	Biotite	Muscovite	Chlorite	Epidote	Hematite stain	Hematite grains	Magnetite	Primary calcite	Secondary calcite	Chert	Schist fragments	Sherd fragments	Microfossils	Chaff
Lydian mold-made Architectural Terracottas																					
TC 11	T63.9:4994	1	■	■	Tr		Tr	■	■			■	■	■			Tr	Tr	Tr		
TC 12	NoEx 73.37	3	■	■	Tr		Tr	■	■	■		■	■				■				
TC 13	T59.9:1400	2	■	■	Tr		Tr	■	Tr	Tr		■	■	■	Tr	Tr					
TC 14	69	8	■	■	Tr			■		■	Tr	■	■				Tr		■		
TC 15	79	1	■	■	Tr			■	■	■	Tr	■	■	■	Tr		Tr				
TC 16	89	2	■	■	Tr			■	■			■	■				■				
TC 17	74	1	■	■			Tr	■	■			■	■				■	■	■		
TC 18	91	3	■	■	Tr			■	■			■	■				Tr	■			
TC 19	93	3	■	■	Tr			■	■	Tr	Tr	■	■	■			Tr	■	Tr		
TC 20	T63.29b:5217	1	■	■	Tr		Tr	■	Tr			■	■					■			Tr
Lydian wheel-made lamps																					
L 1	Uninventoried: HoB 1961	4	■	■			Tr	■	■	Tr	■			Tr			■				
L 2	Uninventoried: HoB 1964	0	■	Tr			Tr	■	■	Tr	■				Tr						
L 3	L65.16: 6813	0	Tr	■				■	■		■				Tr	■					
L 5	Uninventoried: PN 1965	1	■	■				■	■			■	■	Tr				Tr			
L 7	Uninventoried: HoB 1962	4	■	■				■	Tr			■	■	■		Tr		Tr	■		
L 9	Uninventoried: HoB 1961	1	■	■	Tr		Tr	■	■			■	Tr						■		
L 11	L59.81:2067	4	■	■	Tr			■	■			■	■	Tr	■	■					
Typical Sardis ceramic mineral assemblage		2	■	■	Tr			■	■	Tr	Tr	■	■				Tr	Tr	Tr		

of post-firing secondary calcite), or chaff. All samples, except for sample TC 14, contain less than 5% coarse mineral fraction in thin section.

One sample, TC 14, is slightly different in its higher percent coarse fraction (8%), its lack of muscovite mica, and the presence of sherd grog. These differ-ences, however, may be classed as technological, not compositional, as they do not involve any material foreign to the site. There is no strong evidence that this sample was imported.

The mineral assemblages of seven Sardis Lydian wheel-made lamp fragments made during the same period are also shown in Table 2. They also conform to the typical Sardian mineral assemblage, and although they show minor textural differences resulting from the different method of forming, they are nearly identical in composition to the terracottas.

In short, nine of the ten terracotta samples represent a uniform group in terms of composition and manufacture. All ten pastes are characterized by traces of quartz, feldspar, and mica in a matrix of finer mica and fused ground mass, and were probably made at the site. There is no compositional difference between them and contemporary wheel-made lamps or the great bulk of Sardian ceramics previously studied.

White slip from two terracotta samples and from one piece of Lydian pottery were analyzed on an automated Mac-5 electron microprobe programmed with the Geolab system running at 15 kV accelerating voltage, $.03\mu\text{Å}$ beam current, and counting time of 30 sec. Silicate and oxide glasses, and pure metals from the collection in the Department of Earth and Planetary Sciences at MIT were used as standards. Sample preparation involved setting a chip of white slip in epoxy on a glass slide, then carbon coating it. This method often did not produce the highly polished surface required for good analysis, and occasionally low oxide totals resulted; however, since at this stage we merely wanted relative values and indications of presence or absence of an element, the data were satisfactory.

The results are very simple (Table 3), and show the three slips to be similar, each containing abundant Ca, Si, and Al, with varying amounts of K, Fe, and Mg. Unfortunately, because the samples were inadequate to prepare thin sections, it was impossible to determine the mineral form of these elements; however, the composition suggests a clay mineral, muscovite or feldspar base (K, Al, Si) with surprisingly high amounts of Mg, Fe, and Ca. The Ca may have been added as finely ground white calcite, but the reason for the Fe and Mg is unclear as they do not effect the color. Without further information, it remains possible that the Mg, Fe, and Ca were precipitated by accident, post-firing and during burial. In any case, the similarity of slip compositions indicates a technical consistency suggestive of local manufacture and identity of slips used on contemporary terracotta and pottery.

Arrangement of the Catalogue

The finds in the catalogue have been arranged first by functional category and next by subject, and in chronological order within that category. In view of the fragmentary nature of the material, many pieces have been included in an overall category of sima although frequently it is not absolutely defined. If we accept the premise that many of the terracottas come from buildings whose roofing arrangements do not correspond to the pure functional forms that we are accustomed to from the literature, then we must either use existing terms inaccurately, to some degree, or invent a whole new system of terms, which our evidence may not support in the face of close critical inquiry. I have chosen the first alternative, proceeding as if every flat, figured piece were from a sima, either lateral or pedimental, unless there is clear evidence to the contrary.

The large divisions are, then, *sima, antefix* (decorated cover tile), *pantile* (cf. Orlandos I 83f., figs. 56, 57). Sima is used to include all fragments of decorative frieze of which the face must have been set more or less vertically *vis à vis* the observer, whether associated with a roof totally covered with tiles or not. Antefix has a small variety of forms but proportionally more examples; for this reason only the most typical or best preserved have been selected for description or illustration. Of pantiles even fewer examples are included. Few fragments were inventoried unless they had particularly striking features preserved, such as the red, black, or white paint found on **102** through **107** (cf. *ATK*, 68f., fig. 20:1, 2). Several others were saved but add very little to our knowledge of Greek or provincial (Lydian) roof systems or decorations. Most of them are of the Corinthian type, where more or less rectangular tiles are put side by side and the gap protected by a narrow cover tile, which acts like a miniature gabled roof in diverting the rainwater. There are also some examples of what is called a hybrid type

Table 3. Elemental composition of white slips on architectural terracottas from Sardis. Electron microprobe analyses were in oxide weight percent, but elements are shown here as present or absent. "Tr" = trace.

Sample	Catalogue or inventory no.	Color	Mg	Sn	Sb	Ti	V	Mn	Fe	Co	Ni	Cu	Zn	Pb	Na	K	Ca	Si	Al
LP 5	P69.55a:8003	White	■						■							Tr	■	■	■
TC 6	22	White	■						■							■	■	■	■
TC 9	24	White	■						■							■	■	■	■

(*ATK*, 68, figs. 20:3, 64:4), where a long side of the pantile has a curved linking edge that does away with the need for separate cover tiles. One might speculate that the rarity of this type corresponds to the greater difficulty of making and storing it safely.

The use of sima tiles or plaques does not require, in my view, that the whole expanse of roof be tiled, but the use of antefixes does. This means that the first series of antefixes is much later than the introduction of sima tiles at Sardis. We can now see in a general way the relationship of different architectural terracottas to the roof or wall, but particular questions of function or style are discussed in detail in the following catalogue. A short introduction spells out the criteria for classifying the pieces among subgroups of the larger categories mentioned above, and the list is then presented. References to comparative material, especially where there are illustrations, are carried, parenthetically, in the text while occasional explanations and multiple citations are to be found in notes below the entries.

CATALOGUE

Simas

Within the category of simas there are three main groupings:

1. those where humans form part of the subject matter;
2. those where animals are the subjects;
3. those composed largely of decorative patterns, offered for their own sake or as borders for unidentified subjects.

In cases where more than one group is represented, humans take precedence over animals and both take precedence over patterns. In cases where there is implied representation of human figures, as in the case of a chariot wheel with a horse's hoof (**8**) or the griffin at the end of a chariot pole (**9**), the piece is included in group 1 but cross-referenced in the index.

1 *Figs. 30–32*. T63.49:5572. Human head. 600–575.
H. 0.10; W. 0.095; max. Th. (at border) 0.025; Th. of
    relief 0.015.
HoB W10-13/S107-108 *99.6-99.2.

A human head with layered wig, facing left, is in the upper right corner (left side of fragment) of a relief plaque. Upper edge and right side original; other edges

broken. The nose is at the extreme left of the piece. The paint is almost worn off, but there are traces of black at the back of the head, on the waved layers of the hair, and on the frets of the maeander border at the top; there was a red band between this border and the background.

The piece was broken and repaired in antiquity. In fact it must have happened during construction, before firing, as can be seen from the small triangular area at the top right hand corner where the channels of the relief maeander have been filled in. Mends made after firing need either glue or rivets; to act as its own bonding medium the clay body must be green. The fact that the frets were not picked out in paint indicates that the accident happened after the regular painting stage, adding weight to the opinion that the coloring with slip was done before firing in normal practice.

The modeling of this piece is exceptionally fine, and there is evidence of careful tooling around the mouth and nostril (Fig. 32). On the basis of style the head should be placed in the first quarter of the sixth century since it shares some characteristics, such as the ear and hair, with small bronze statuettes from Samos (Richter, *Kouroi*, 22–23, figs. 117–122, Sounion group), and some, such as the profile and general swing of the eyebrows, with a small marble piece in London (ibid., 39, figs. 151–153, Orchomenos-Thera group).

2 *Frontispiece and Fig. 33*. T60.35:2914. MANISA 1673.
    Head of a bearded Lydian. Ca. 560.
H. 0.08; W. 0.05; Th. 0.03, of background 0.02.
PN room B, S at W251.7/S377.5 *87.00.

The head and shoulders of this Lydian man appear to have been chipped away from a larger composition so that we have nothing but the figure itself to work from. We can tell that the head is from an architectural terracotta from the slight remains of the background, in particular those on the right side of the face.

His hair is black and arranged like a layered wig falling just over the shoulder. His face is white, the profile outlined in black. Black also serves for indicating the details of his face, eye, ear, and beard. The eye is modeled as an oval which is outlined in black over white, and the pupil is a black circle. Above is the line of the eyebrow, which joins the line of the nose and forehead.

The ear, too, is modeled in a general way and its edges picked out in a simple hook pattern which is immediately complicated by a pendent spiral which forms an elegant earring.

The beard has a scalloped upper edge but leaves a considerable area of the jaw and the lower chin shaven —a Lydian fashion for muttonchop whiskers?

He is wearing a red tunic with a black maeander border and a very elegant sleeve pattern which cannot be reconstructed with certainty. It seems to have been made up of red maeanders and white diamonds framed in black. In sum, one might say that he richly deserves the title of Lydian Dandy which has been informally bestowed upon him. This is to continue the Greek view of the Lydians as luxury-loving and effete. The earrings are mentioned by Xenophon (*Anab.* 3.1.31) and the rich clothing by several authors. This includes bright colored headbands, gold-woven chitons, purple quilts, and red blankets.

Since the head is detached from its original surroundings we can only guess at the overall design. Perhaps he is a horseman, one of the officers of the famous Lydian cavalry on parade. The reasoning for this suggestion lies in his relative smallness as the terracottas go and an indication in the modeling that his right arm is moving forwards as if to hold the reins. In this connection one might cite the limestone relief slab from Bin Tepe (the royal burial mounds of Sardis) in the British Museum (*Sardis* R2 [1978] no. 231; Pryce, 99–101, fig. 164) which shows a file of horsemen whose upper bodies are remarkably like that of the piece under discussion. A comparable but later and cruder series of riders is found on terracotta revetments from Düver in southwest Asia Minor, near modern Burdur.

Published: *BASOR* 162, 26f., fig. 15; Hanfmann, *Letters,* pl. II; M. Renard, "À propos de quelques oeuvres de l'archaisme étrusque," *Hommages à Albert Grenier* III, *Collection Latomus* 58 (1962) 1299–1314, pl. 245:5. For the rich textiles of the Lydians see Sappho, who sings of a bright-colored headband from Sardis, F219(98) 1–3, 10–12 = *Sardis* M2 (1972) no. 139; Johannes Laurentius Lydus mentions "gold-woven chitons," *De Magistratibus Populi Romani* 3.64. Plato the comic poet, quoted in Athenaeus *Deipnosophistae* 2.48b, describes the Lydians as "reclining in finery on couches with ivory feet, with purple-dyed coverlets and red Sardis blankets, *Sardis* M2 (1972) no. 128. See also the article by C. H. Greenewalt, Jr. and L. J. Majewski, "Lydian Textiles" in "Memorial Volume for R. S. Young," ed. K. DeVries, forthcoming.

The Düver architectural terracottas came on the art market in the mid-sixties (Sotheby Sale, Feb. 24, 1964, cat. lots 50–64, and July 6, 1964, cat. lots 45–56) but were recognized as coming from Asia Minor and as

being of Phrygian type (*ATK*, xiii and 218 with extensive references and figs. 70–70a). Many more similar and associated pieces were collected by the staff of the Burdur Museum and are discussed by W. W. Cummer, "Phrygian Roof Tiles in the Burdur Museum," *Anatolia* 14:4 (1970) 29ff.

3 *Fig. 30.* NOEX 73.3. Human head. Ca. 550.
H. 0.13 (top edge is original); W. 0.12; Th. 0.057 (including border), of background 0.018.
From the Northeast Wadi, somewhat above the sector excavated in 1969 (Fig. 2 No. 16; actually found by Yuksel Karakoc's cow).

A fragment with the upper part of a human head (facing left) preserved and a maeander pattern above it. Both the maeander design and the head are in relief and were originally black. The head shows very sensitive modeling even though it is rather worn. To the left of the nose a small piece in high relief remains, which seems to be part of the figure's hand.

This head is very large in relation to the piece as a whole. Its preserved height is ca. 0.04 m., and the total height of well preserved sima tiles is usually about 0.20 m. This unusual proportion precludes the use of a standing figure in the design and makes a reclining banqueter or a musician a likely subject. Schemes from Larisa on the Hermus and Etruria afford the best general equivalents, but an exact comparison is wanting.

Published: *BASOR* 215, 55f., fig. 24. For parallels from Larisa and Etruria see *Larisa* II 64f., pls. 22–33; *ATK*, pls. 28–29; Östenberg, 168.

4 *Fig. 34.* T61.78:3769. MANISA. Human holding a sphinx or griffin by the tail, "Potnia Theron." Mid-6th C.
H. 0.11, of preserved figure 0.055; W. 0.16; Th. at top border 0.047.
PN S380/W245 *88.65.

A roughly rectangular piece; the original upper edge is preserved but other three sides are broken. The upper border is composed of a row of equilateral triangles in relief (L. of side 0.03) which are painted in white slip and have a thick red stripe at the bottom. The effect created is a row of alternating upright and inverted triangles. Above this is a plain relief band, now much abraded.

The sphinx is facing to the left, the figure to the right. The paint from the top surface of the figures is worn away but enough remains to reconstruct black and white stripes for the wing of the sphinx and red for its body. The hair of the figure, a god or goddess, is painted black and falls in a straight line to the shoulder without additional modeling in three dimensions, while the ear and eye were brought out by modeling as well as paint. It is very probable that the tunic of the figure was checked—the divisions being picked out with fine black lines such as we see in the terracotta published by Greenewalt ("Exhibitionist," pl. 8–15) and in **2,** the "Lydian Dandy." The use of this fine black line is continued in the outlining of the hand holding the tail of the beast. The torso is seen in three-quarter view and the figure's left arm is seen beyond. It seems very likely that the composition was symmetrical.

Published: *BASOR* 166, 24, fig. 18; 215, 55, fig. 23.

5 *Figs. 35–36.* NOEX 71.16. Fighting men. Mid-6th C.
H. 0.10; W. 0.21; Th. 0.04, of background 0.025.
Found on surface ca. 20 m. NW of PC, where village track for wheeled traffic (ca. W250/S580) descends to the river.

We see a considerable part of the bodies of two combattants and what is probably the hand of a third. At the left a swordsman staggering backwards is thrusting his sword upwards towards his enemy, whose hand is the only part of his body to be seen. To the right is a bowman wearing a tall bow case and quiver and a Phrygian cap or animal mask. He has drawn back his elbow and appears to be shooting towards the right. One is reminded of Greek representations of battles between gods and giants or between Greeks and Amazons.

The piece is much worn, but some of the color scheme can be recaptured: the bowman's arm and cap were black, his bow case red. The layered hair of the hoplite was black and so were his skirt and legs. The breastplate was red and the pommel of his sword was black; the opponent's hand was black.

The modeling of the figures is bold, but one misses the sensitivity shown in some of the terracottas.

This is the only piece from Sardis to have more than two principal figures not separated by a border. One wonders how it was arranged on the roof; whether there were other linking groups to create the illusion of a large-scale battle or whether the composition of this piece allowed it to be repeated without adding other groups to it.

It has been suggested (by C. H. Greenewalt, Jr.) that the subject is of Theseus and the minotaur. The argu-

ment is based largely on the position of the fragmentary hand on the left and its similarity to the terracotta piece from Sardis in the Metropolitan Museum of Art, New York (*Sardis* X [1926] 9f., pl. II; *ATK,* pl. 37). But there are two important difficulties: first the fact that "Theseus" is armed and second that the presence, on the right, of the bowman without a division between the figures is not part of the usual compositional scheme.

6 *Fig. 37.* T60.30:2879. Human knee and calf. Late 6th C.
W. 0.08, of under-face 0.06; H. 0.07; L. of leg 0.06.
PN room B (general area W248-260/S370-380) *89.00-88.25.

This is part of a scene which included a kneeling figure in relief, facing left, of which just the knee and the calf are preserved. The subject was possibly an archer preparing to shoot, such as we have, partially preserved, on **5.** The piece probably had a lower border of rectangular section and was painted solid red on the underside. This is what makes it certain that the figure to which the knee belongs was represented as kneeling, but there is no indication where in the frame this figure was placed. The whole piece is on a small scale and there is delicate modeling at the knee. Only the white slip underpainting is visible on the figure. The background seems to have been white, and there is a red band at the junction of the bottom molding and the vertical face.

7 *Fig. 38.* T74.1:8300. Fragment of chariot hunting group. Mid-6th C.
H. 0.11; W. 0.11; Th. 0.022, with relief 0.026-0.025.
AcN W180-184.5/N99-101.50 *391.60-391.25.

The piece is broken on all sides and only a little of the back surface remains; this was painted red, at least towards the bottom. The forequarters of a galloping horse and the upper part of a running dog are preserved. Shoulder and forelegs of horse are red and the neck and mane white; back portion of the body is black. All the preserved parts of the dog are red with details added in black except for a small speck of white. The horse is in harness for drawing a chariot; a loose part of the traces curves down in relief just behind the foreleg and is continued in black paint above it. Black details on white at the root of the neck are largely lost but can be reconstructed as extra parts of the harness (cf. *Sardis* X [1926] frontispiece and fig.

11; *ATK*, pl. 39.1., now lost). This motif is common at Larisa (*Larisa* II 31–53, pl. 1–14) but rare at Sardis.

8 *Fig. 39.* T61.44:3481. Chariot wheel. 6th C.
H. 0.05; W. 0.108; Th. 0.025.
PN W270/S355 *87.23.

Lower part of four-spoked chariot wheel and horse's hoof to right. The tire of the wheel is brought out by three stripes of golden brown paint. The lower border is painted in alternating oblongs of black and white (H. 0.02; L. 0.025). The underside of this piece shows traces of a pattern of black diamonds on a white background, part of a much-used decorative motif.

9 *Fig. 40.* T63.34:5278. Small griffin head. Ca. 550.
H. 0.09; W. 0.095; Th. of border 0.025, of panel 0.02.
HoB W10/S102.8 *99.5 (under 99.6 floor).

The fragment is in the shape of an irregular inverted triangle in whose apex is a small head of a griffin in relief. Above the griffin is a wide maeander border (W. 0.068) whose top forms the original upper edge of the piece. The frets of the maeander are in relief and picked out in black paint against a white background. The head of the griffin, which is facing right, is painted in black and red, much of which has worn off. The scale of the head is such that it can hardly have formed the subject of a plaque in its own right but must be associated with the customary finial ornament of a chariot pole. (Cf. *Larisa* II passim; *ATK*, 45–66, pls. 19–34). Since the griffin's head as a representation of a traditional ornament should be regarded as stylistically stationary and therefore not a reliable chronological indicator, we should estimate the date of this piece on technical grounds to be about 550 or later.

10 *Fig. 41.* T62.42:4770. Small bird. Ca. 550.
H. 0.07; W. at border 0.053; max. Th. 0.033.
PN area 3 level VI, ca. W230-240/S370-380 ca. *86.40.

The body of the bird is covered with red slip over white base. The wing is white, outlined in black.

This piece seems to have been converted from a minor subject as a relief on a frieze or sima like those from Mylasa (*ATK*, 116, fig. 35 and pl. 59:1) to what amounts to a freestanding statuette. It does in fact stand on its own and has sufficient thickness to be convincing although the back is not modeled. We cannot tell whether this was intended as ornament, toy, or vo-

tive offering. The same sort of thing seems to have happened to the "Lydian Dandy," **2**.

11 *Fig. 42.* T61.76:3737. Bird's legs. 2nd half 6th C.
H. 0.09; W. 0.117; Th. 0.021, at border 0.033.
HoB platform E2/S96 *99.30-99.00.

Lower legs and lower part of the tail of a bird strutting to the right. The identification of the subject as a bird is made conclusive by the well-modeled claws which can be seen resting on the lower border. They were covered by a stripe of red paint, some of which still adheres, although almost all the piece is now bare of paint.

As in **27**, the presence of a nail hole—this time complete—shows that this was an ornamental plaque. The condition of our piece does not allow us to speculate very widely, but it is tempting to think of a scene such as those with "quail" on the terracottas from Mylasa (*ATK*, 116, fig. 35 and pl. 59:1). The legs and feet, however, are similar to those of the owls on early Athenian coins (*BMC* Attica, 23f.).

12 *Figs. 43–44.* T61.86:3862. Fragment of boar's head
and shoulder. Ca. 580.
H. 0.098; W. 0.085; Th. 0.033 (max.), 0.023 (min.).
HoB W4/S91 *99.00.

This piece has no original edges; the back face is finished and there are horizontal striations but no paint. The color is wholly red over a buff slip and there are no traces of black (red = Munsell 2.5YR5/6; buff = 10YR7/3, "very pale brown"). Perhaps this darker slip accounts for the duller impression of color given by this fragment.

The most striking feature of this piece is the treatment of the eye and the ear—they combine to give a strong impression of a griffin. Upon reflection, however, one realizes that griffins' knobs do not normally have feather-like grooves beside them, that the head is usually free of the body, and there is nothing behind until the wing is reached. It is the presence of the several modeled forms behind and below the eye that makes certain the identification of this piece as a boar.

Boars are rare as subjects for architectural terracottas; they are not infrequent however on Wild Goat Style pottery and on Attic, where the Gorgon Painter and Kleitias furnish the best parallels (cf. *AH*, pls. 35, 42; Cook, pl. 18, 19A). With these comparisons in mind, together with the general stratigraphy of the sector, a date of about 580 seems an appropriate estimate.

Compare a boar on a ring from Sardis and one on a metope from the Sikyonian Treasury at Delphi, which is particularly close.

I am grateful to Crawford H. Greenewalt, Jr., for his identification of this subject and insistence upon it in the early stages of this study. For a boar on an architectural terracotta see *ATK*, 206, no. 3, fig. 66.3, one of a group of sima fragments which were on the art market in 1965. For the boar on a ring from Sardis see *Sardis* XIII (1925) no. 98, pls. 9:11, 11:4; clearer illustration in J. Boardman, *Greek Gems and Finger Rings* (New York 1972) pl. 292 and ref. to idem, "Pyramidal Stamp Seals in the Persian Empire," *Iran* 8 (1970) pl. 8, 195. For Sikyonian boar see Richter, *Sculpture*, fig. 358 (her date 575–550), with reference to T. Homolle ed., *Fouilles de Delphes* IV, *Monuments figurés* (1909–1931) pl. III and p. 22.

13 *Fig. 45.* T64.8:5990. Bull's hoof. Ca. 575–550.
H. 0.09; W. 0.063; Th. 0.025.
HoB W17-25/S116-120 *99.80-99.60.

A bull's hoof over a maeander border. Almost all the paint has disappeared except for traces of red over white on the bottom part of the hoof. The modeled surfaces are not much battered but offer little opportunity to estimate the overall quality of the lost portion.

This is the only example we have found in our group of terracottas which has a bovine subject. Since the hoof is tucked under the upper leg (now lost), we should reconstruct a group of a bull brought to its knees by a lion or other fierce beast.

14 *Frontispiece and Fig. 46.* T62.13:4389. MANISA.
Dog running. Ca. 550–530.
H. 0.09; W. 0.13; Th. of face 0.026.
HoB E5/S90 *98.50.

The dog is drawn in much simplified outline with gray paint (Munsell N3). The relief, too, is simplified and there is very little modeling; the pose is that of the "flying gallop" and similar in general impression to that on a hunting frieze from Larisa (*Larisa* II pl. 9:27; *ATK*, pl. 23:1). The dog is running to the left and is placed more or less horizontally just above the lower border which is broken off in a straight line across the bottom of the fragment. The back legs and haunches are not preserved. The feeling is reminiscent of the swinging line of Protocorinthian dogs.

Besides the outlining of the form, the body is di-

vided arbitrarily into box-like sections with painted lines; these correspond roughly to the head, neck, and midsection, while the forelegs form another unit. The head and midsection are filled with bright orangy spots. Neck and forelegs were probably painted in solid color but the use of spots can not be definitely ruled out. This use of outline and spotted filling ornament strengthens the link between Lydian art and East Greek art in general, especially Rhodian and Fikellura pottery. There are traces of black and white paint on the under edge.

For Protocorinthian dogs see Cook, pl. 10A; also idem, "Fikellura Pottery," *BSA* 34 (1933–34) pl. 4a. See also C. H. Greenewalt, Jr., "Fikellura and 'Early Fikellura' Pottery from Sardis," *California Studies in Classical Antiquity* 4 (1971) 153–180.

15 *Fig. 47.* T63.42:5379. Seated griffin. Mid-6th C.
W. 0.14; H. 0.12; Th. 0.033, of background 0.016.
PN W234-237/S342-345 *88.85-88.30.

There are no original edges but the back surface is smoothed. On the face is part of the rounded body of a griffin (or a sphinx), facing right, set obliquely (lower left to upper right) with right foreleg slanting down to lower right corner of fragment. A tiny portion of the left foreleg reaching upwards can be seen above this. The wing extends more or less horizontally to the left side of the piece. The junction of the wing and the body can be seen between the body and the right foreleg in the form of a black stripe and a large knob in relief. The body of the monster is red over white slip, the background white. The last row of feathers at the lower edge of the wing is white with a thin border of black and towards the top of the wing there seem to have been transverse lines making a light check pattern. The line of the join between the neck and the wing can be made out at the top of the piece, directly above the junction of the leg and the body.

16 *Fig. 47.* T65.2:6627. Seated griffin. Mid-6th C.
W. 0.085; H. 0.14; Th. 0.018, with relief 0.035.
PN W285-287/S325-327 *87.3.

No original edges are preserved and the back is plain and smoothed. Only the wing, stump of one leg, and part of the body are preserved. The surface is abraded and most of the paint is lost except for some red on the leg and body and some black on the wing. The wing is clearly differentiated into rows of feathers along its length by having the edges vertical and the faces oblique in relief.

On the back, at the top, is a set of two parallel striations which corresponds well to a similar set below, and they are the primary indications that the griffin is seated. Close comparison with calipers at several equivalent points on the bodies shows that this piece comes from the same mold as **15**.

17 *Fig. 48*. T59.45:2024. Head, neck, and forequarters of a griffin. Early 6th C.
H. 0.15; W. 0.107; Th. 0.023.
BS W 13, W54-57/S1.50-4.00 *94.50-94.00.

This comes from a relatively large-scale griffin, which must have formed the subject of the plaque, as opposed to the small-scale griffin heads which are the standard ornaments for the finials of chariot poles (cf. **9**). Noteworthy is the painting of the upper beak, the remains of a painted triskeles just to the left of the jaws, and the check pattern, as of a light Scottish tartan, at the neck. The modeling is perfunctory compared to some examples but the coloring compensates for it in some degree.

18 *Fig. 49*. T61.83:3809. MANISA. Horse's head. Before 550.
H. 0.067; W. 0.06; Th. 0.03.
HoB E5/S95 *99.30.

Upper part of horse's head and mane. This piece has suffered from over firing or re-firing in a reducing atmosphere, and the whole of the body has consequently turned gray (Munsell N4/0). It is nonetheless clear that this fragment comes from what must have been one of the most carefully finished architectural terracottas at Sardis. In addition to the usual color scheme, now almost all lost, the details of the head and its equipment were picked out and retouched with a sharp tool. This includes fine lines on the molded locks of the mane and a very crisp representation of the bridle straps and cheek pieces. The forelock is less carefully worked and could possibly be a decorative tassel. The horse's eye is done in the human form, as is common in sixth century vase painting. The upper border is broken off, but there are some traces of red paint at the division between it and the background, which was originally white. Hanfmann has seen that this must be a ridden, rather than a chariot horse because the head does not form one of a pair.

Published: *BASOR* 166, 14, fig. 9.

19 *Frontispiece and Fig. 50*. T62.5:4212. MANISA 1675. Winged horse.
H. 0.16; W. 0.210; Th. 0.023, max. with relief 0.035.
AcT E7.5/N21 *402.8.

This sima tile with a little of the left edge of the spout preserved shows a lively winged horse (Pegasos) prancing. It corresponds to the piece (found by the first Sardis expedition in 1922) illustrated by Shear (*Sardis* X [1926] pl. IX) which formed a corner between the lateral and a raking sima. In our piece, however, the horse is leaping well beyond the outer edge of the spout and seems likely to meet his opposite number in midstream.

Figure 51 shows a modern terracotta reconstruction made at Sardis by Eric Hostetter from impressions of original pieces and painted with material which would have been available to the Lydians. It is part of an attempt to recreate at the site the impression made by the pieces in their unbroken and unworn condition.

The horse's head and forequarters are outlined in black. The near leg is black and the far one red. Details within the outline of the head are also picked out in black (nostril, eye, eyebrow); the open mouth is modeled and so is the forelock. At the right, a black horizontal line the end of which curls downward in front of Pegasos' eye may well be part of a painted triskeles used to fill the gap above the spout. The mane is painted black and shown as ragged but in large locks. An echo of this is painted red within the area of the neck while the rest of the neck is white. The forepart of the wing is black and the rear is divided by red bars alternating with white and separated by black lines. The belly and hindquarters are solid red with some streaking. At the left of the spout there are painted two small shiny red dots as if to emphasize the spout.

Following Shear and **21** and **22** we might reconstruct the vertical face with a chevron border at the top and a plain one below, which would give us a reconstructed height for the sima of ca. 0.21.

Published: *BASOR* 170, 32, fig. 22; Hanfmann, *Letters*, fig. 71.

20 *Fig. 52*. T68.17:7830. Pair of walking horses. Ca. 575.
H. 0.121; W. 0.158; Th. 0.04.
PN W261.5/S341 *86.00.

Two joining fragments which form the hind legs and underbelly of two large animals, whose mid-legs at least are reminiscent of a cow. The pair is established by the doubling of the legs. For the species of the animal, horses or monsters seem most likely as draught animals, which is what I take these for. I see them as the more stately kind of chariot horses used for formal processions, especially weddings or assemblies of the gods. Where the surface is preserved, the body was painted black; the surface is distinctly flaky and cracked, as if it had been subjected to considerable heat. The piece should be dated on stratigraphic grounds between 575 and 560 since it was found in the middle of the gold refining area in PN.

For horses in processions cf. Attic amphora from the Piraeus, Corinthian krater by the Three Maidens Painter (name piece), and the procession of gods on the François vase (Richter, *Handbook*[6] fig. 441f. *AH*, pl. XI, 40–41). For the gold refining area in PN see A. Ramage in *BASOR* 199, 16–28; Hanfmann-Waldbaum, 310–315; Hanfmann, *Letters*, 230–234, figs. 172–179; A. Ramage, "Gold Refining at the time of the Lydian Kings of Sardis," *Proceedings of the X International Congress of Classical Archaeology* (forthcoming); S. M. Goldstein in *BASOR* 228, 54–57.

21 *Fig. 53*. T61.6:3176. Hindquarters of prancing horse. Ca. 550.
H. 0.173; W. 0.13. Horse: H. 0.09; Th. 0.09.
HoB W10/S90 *101.80.

Painted black on white background. The horse is represented as having its rear legs on the ground, formed by the plain but much abraded lower border of the terracotta (cf. *Sardis* X [1926] fig. 15). The original underside is preserved and shows a design of diamonds, which is shared by **22**. In fact the horses, although of different colors, seem to come from the same mold in so far as their dimensions and attitude correspond exactly.
Cf. *BASOR* 215, 56 and fig. 26; *Sardis* X (1926) pl. X and 32f.; *ATK*, no. 10, fig. 21.

22 *Fig. 53*. T63.22:5169. Rear legs of horse. Ca. 550.
H. 0.085; W. 0.105; Th. 0.08.
HoB E5/S110-115 to *99.30 floor.

This is much battered but almost certainly comes from the same mold and possibly even the same frieze as **21**. This conclusions is supported by the close similarity of the dimensions of the legs and the patterns on the undersides of both pieces. The chief difference from **21** is the fact that this horse was red rather than black. It is by no means unknown to alternate colors on friezes (cf. *Sardis* X [1926] pls. IX, X; *ATK*, 71,

nos. 7, 8). This appears to be the lower left corner of a lateral sima, since the left edge is original and the painted underside very wide.

23 *Fig. 54*. NOEX 73.6. Head of roaring lion.
H. 0.105; L. 0.15; Th. 0.03, with relief 0.04; W. of border 0.048.

Top part of a sima with maeander border in relief and the head of a roaring lion facing right. The top edge is smoothed and painted with brownish red bands. The surface of the maeander is lustrous black or sometimes brown, as in the Lydian pottery known as streaked ware. The lion itself is modeled in relief and its outline and inner details are boldly emphasized in black paint, which makes a strong contrast with the white of the background and of the head. The teeth, for instance, and the eye and ear are not merely painted on but have decisive shape in the modeling of the relief. There is a strong possibility that there was a painted knob just above the relief portion of the lion's nose as in the supposed coins of Alyattes and other representations, but exposure to the elements and the growth of lichen has made it very difficult to tell. Close inspection at the broken edge to the right of the lion's nose shows several specks of black paint in an oblique configuration. This allows us to reconstruct a group of two lions in defiant opposition or (perhaps more likely) a single lion roaring at this own tail in the manner of the lion group from Akalan, near the Black Sea coast (*ATK*, pls. 61, 62). The chief reason for preferring the latter is that in such an arrangement the head can be seen more clearly and is not masked by the spout from a viewer on the ground.

For coins of Alyattes see *BMC* Lydia; Hogarth, *Ephesus*, Atlas, pls. I, II; A. R. Bellinger in Robinson *Essays*, 10–15, pl. I; Oleson, pls. 1a, 2; Münzen and Medaillen, list 335 (June 1972) no. 1. For the knob esp. see E. S. G. Robinson, *JHS* 71 (1951) 159–161, referred to in Bellinger, ibid.

24 *Figs. 55–56*. T62.1:4127. Striding lions. Ca. 580–550.
H. 0.13, of triangles with painted band 0.045; W. 0.155, of ledge at top 0.035; L. of lion 0.085.
PN ca. W220/S370 surface.

The surface of the piece is divided almost exactly in half by a decorative upper border and a row of lions. The upper border consists of a plain molding and a series of triangles in relief which are painted in white slip and have an orangy-red stripe at the bottom. As in **4**, the effect created is of a row of alternating upright and inverted triangles. The lions seem to have been set in pairs, confronting one another (see reconstruction drawing, Fig. 56). This results in an arrangement where the animals alternate between head to head and rump to rump position. Besides one well preserved lion, approximately in the center of the piece, we have the hindquarters of another at the left and faint but clear indications of yet another at the right in the short oblique lines in relief at the upper corner. These lines seem to be a simplified way of rendering the lion's mane, and one might wonder whether such a representation was intended to convey something of the ferocity of the beast, since unreal rays frequently project from the noses of archaic lions both in this medium and others (see **23** for references).

It is possible that the creature on the right, whose presence is implied by the rays in relief similar to those of the lion's mane, is a boar rather than another lion, and we see a series of simplified bristles presented in the same spirit as the lion's mane. The possibility is introduced because the rays of the lion's nose do not match the rays emanating from the unknown beast. Either this is an unimportant piece of carelessness or it must be taken seriously as an indicator of a different animal subject in the frieze.

The color scheme on this piece is garish, with much use of a shiny orangy-red; the uppermost molding is painted wholly in that color and the upright triangles alternate between white and orange, having a broad stripe to form their bases. Of the central, and largely preserved, lion the head is black, the body, forelegs, and the forward (left) hind leg red, and the tail and right hindquarter black. Of the other lion (left), the tail and left hindquarter are black; the right leg is red. The background is white.

The details are finished in too crude a manner for one to be dogmatic about the dating, but the overall form seems to bear a resemblance to what R. M. Cook calls "Ripe Corinthian" lions (Cook, fig. 6, opp. p. 50).

25 *Fig. 57.* T61.65:3626. Hindquarters of lion. Before 550.
H. 0.064; W. 0.097; Th. 0.014, with relief 0.035.
PN W250/S375 ca. *86.85.

Original left hand edge with lion striding to right. The black paint is much worn on the top surface. The tail curls up strongly over the back.

This piece is dated on stratigraphic grounds; its level is associated with the bottom courses of Lydian walls thought to have been built shortly after the Persian sack and occupation of Sardis in 547 B.C. and hence frequently referred to as Persian (*BASOR* 162, 26f.; *BASOR* 166, 20f.). This piece may well be a relic of the destruction.

26 *Fig. 58.* T65.9:6691. Hindquarters of rampant lion. Ca. 550.
H. 0.095; L. 0.12; Th. 0.016. 0.034 overall.
PN W288/S325 *86.46.

Much abraded on top surface but paint and modeling remains where the relief met the background. The positioning of legs and tail is like that on a large tile from Sardis found in 1911 and now in the Metropolitan Museum of Art, New York. Even closer is the body of a lion found in 1911, on the Lydian Terrace, not far from the piece already cited. Unfortunately this piece is lost and it is therefore difficult to compare the two because the published photograph is poor (*Sardis* X [1926] no. 5, fig. 6; *ATK*, 73, 14, pl. 43:3).

Justification for its restoration as standing obliquely comes from the relation of the relief to the general run of the striations on the back. Stratification and context indicate a date in the middle of the sixth century.

For Metropolitan Museum lion see *Sardis* I (1922) 77, ill. 73; T. L. Shear, *AJA* 27 (1923) 141, fig. 6; *ATK*, 72, no. 12, pl. 43:1.

27 *Fig. 59.* T61.61:3591. Lion's paw. 6th C.
H. 0.09; W. 0.10; Th. 0.036.
HoB W5/S105 to *99.30.

Piece of decorative plaque with lion's paw standing on maeander border. The maeander is represented in relief, reinforced by black paint. The channels are painted white. Similarly the paw in relief is painted black and the background is white. A trace of a nail hole half way down the oblique broken surface to the right of the paw indicates that this was a decorative plaque and therefore not part of a gutter sima. One should note that it is rare to find nail holes in the architectural terracottas from Sardis. Dated sixth century by nature and by context, i.e., all pottery in this level was of the sixth century (cf. *Sardis* X [1926] pl. 5).

28 *Figs. 60–61.* T61.90:3902. Seated sphinx. Mid-6th C.

H. 0.12; W. 0.095; Th. 0.024, with relief 0.04.
HoB W4/S86 *99.30 mixed fill along N ramp.

No original edges are preserved and the front surface is much abraded but some details of the paint survive. The figure is seated, looking to the right with its left paw raised. This corresponds in general to the composition of a sima in the Museum of Fine Arts, Boston whose provenience is unknown, in which griffins are shown standing on either side of the spout, pawing a sacred tree (*ATK*, pl. 16:1). It is possible that our piece is a griffin rather than a sphinx since the neck slopes back sharply and is black rather than white. If we take the François vase as a guide (*AH*, pls. 40, 41, and detail 45) we see that both species can share exactly the same body type. In our case I am inclined to think that we have the lower neck before it has changed to the white, bib-like form found on a large fragment from NEW belonging to a Lydian painted pithos imitating the Wild Goat Style (Fig. 130. *BASOR* 199, 35, fig. 24; *Sardis* R1 [1975] fig. 307). On the breast are painted feathers, rows of short tongues with dots in the centers (only a few of these are fully preserved). Schematized feathers are picked out at the root of the wing. The musculature of the upper right foreleg is carefully modeled and outlined in black over white. Whether this is a sphinx or a griffin, it is still a different type from **15** and **16**.

29 *Fig. 62.* NOEX 60.5. MANISA. Winged animal.
H. 0.14; W. 0.102; Th. 0.022; max. Th. 0.027.
Surface 20 m. S of PC (ca. W200/S620).

The wing and part of the body of an animal facing left; there is no way of telling the species since all indicators are broken off. The background is white, the body orangy-red, and the wing alternately black and white on its lower, outside edge and solid white with a narrow black outline on the forward edge. The back edge of the wing is scalloped in relief, as was that of **19**. Anatomical details are painted in black on the body. The front edge of the hind leg shows at the right edge of the relief. The back of the piece has two broad stripes of streaked brown paint.

This is a fine piece where the color is well preserved, but it offers too many opportunities for speculation and has therefore been entitled simply "winged animal."

30 *Fig. 63.* T63.61:5867. Wing of griffin (or sphinx). Ca. 570.

H. 0.105; W. 0.09; Th. 0.035.
HoB W10-13/S110-113 *99.10-98.90.

Almost all the curving upper part of the left wing of a large griffin, perhaps from a scene with two, heraldically confronted (as in *ATK*, pl. 16:1). This is the upper part of the wing where it begins to bend back on itself as if to form a spiral (cf. **29**).

What remains is black, concentrated near five narrow relief bands which indicate rows of feathers. It seems probable to me that the wing was not totally black but that the white below was reserved to provide emphasis. Perhaps there were transverse stripes to further differentiate feathers. The background was white.

This form of the wing tip seems to be early rather than late archaic in mainland Greece but continues in Clazomenian black figure until the third quarter of the sixth century (cf. *CVA* British Museum, pl. 587:13–15, fragments from Tell Defenneh). From the wing alone it is not possible to identify the subject conclusively, but it must be one of these semi-divine or monstrous creatures which so enrich the Orientalizing and archaic periods of Greek art, of which the griffin seems most at home in Lydia.

31 *Figs. 64–66.* T65.13:6810. Spouted sima tile. Last quarter 6th C.
H. 0.165; W. 0.395; P.L. with spout 0.40.
PN W292.6-293.5/S331.3-332.3 *86.54.

This almost complete lateral sima tile has been recomposed from many fragments. It is formed of two friezes with balancing lotus flowers on either side of the spout, surmounted by a band of egg and dart molding. The molding is topped by a narrow unadorned border of rectangular section with traces of red and white paint. The lower border is a plain half-round molding also with traces of paint. Many of the pieces illustrated in *Sardis* X (1926) have some elements like those described here but there is no piece which corresponds exactly.

This piece was found together with many other pieces of roof tiles in a purposely stopped-up well in the densely built-up area of PN. This fact certainly accounts for the almost total lack of paint and the loss of most of the original surface. Early houses in this area date from the later sixth century but habitation seems to have been continuous until the destruction of Sardis by Antiochus III in 213, which may have resulted in the filling of the well, perhaps as a punitive measure against the supporters of his rebellious cousin, Achaeus.

The bold molding of the patterns and the technique of the painting, so far as it is preserved, establish this piece as archaic but there is no reason to regard it as especially early.

For pieces with general similarities see *Sardis* X (1926) nos. 5, 9, 12, 22–23, figs. 9, 22, pls. VII, VIII; also G. M. A. Richter, *Handbook of the Greek Collection, Metropolitan Museum of Art* (Cambridge, Mass. 1953) 44, pl. 31c. The same pieces are collected in *ATK*, pls. 48, 49.

32 *Fig. 67.* UNINVENTORIED 1960. Egg and dart fragment.
H. 0.08; W. 0.09; Th. 0.028-0.033.
Chance find.

The piece comes from a lateral sima; part of the inner face (root) of the spout can be seen at the back. Above are remains of a guilloche band in relief and below that is a narrow band of square section which separates the guilloche from the egg and dart pattern. The eggs appear to alternate between red (left) and black, while the concave dividing loops are white and the convex black. A simplified dart remains white even while projecting from a white background. Above, the high relief is black and the background white. The guilloche pattern in relief is the most interesting feature of the piece since it does not occur like this anywhere else among the Sardis finds. Below the egg and dart, flanking the spout, one might restore balancing lotus flowers as in the foregoing piece (cf. *Sardis* X [1926] fig. 22; *ATK*, pl. 49:1, 2).

33 *Figs. 68–69.* T59.47:2156. Egg and dart molding. Late archaic.
H. 0.05; W. 0.09; Th. 0.04.
BS W54-57/S2.00-4.40 *95.50-95.00.

This piece is from the lower part of the frieze of a decorative sima with an egg and dart pattern both molded and picked out in paint. The eggs seem to have been white and the divisions between them, including the darts, painted in black. These black divisions are not modeled and are generally rather crude. The eggs are decorated with a faint red tongue in the center. The lower edge is painted red and portions of what looks like a black and white diamond pattern are preserved on the underside, Fig. 69. General considerations of technique indicate this piece is archaic, but neither its

findspot nor any specific details give any further assistance in dating.

34 *Fig. 70.* T60.1:2243. Egg and dart molding. Archaic or later.
H. 0.06; W. 0.105; Th. 0.036.
HoB E10/S95 *101.00-100.00.

There are two eggs plastically rendered and separated by a single coil of semicircular section. There is no paint left except on the top and the back.

35 *Figs. 71–72.* T62.24:4491. Egg and dart molding. Late archaic?
H. 0.072; W. 0.177; Th. 0.07.
PN ''Persian West'' (general area W235-245/S375-385) in Hellenistic wall *88.6.

Lower part of a frieze with an egg and dart border set above a plain strip. Two eggs are preserved to their whole width in the center and there are the remains of two others, rather broken, on either side. The color scheme seems to have been one of alternating white and red with the darts and divisions between the eggs brought out in black. On the extreme left, white paint is preserved on the bottom border. To the right the surface is broken away. This fragment is proved to be the bottom of the tile by the extension of the under surface (Fig. 72) and the lack of paint on it. Another piece (NoEx 71.23), with exactly the same profile but with only a few specks of paint and hardly any of the original surface intact, has been omitted from the catalogue.

36 *Figs. 73–74.* T63.11:5021. Egg and dart molding. Late archaic.
H. 0.09; W. 0.088; Th. 0.03.
HoB E5/S115 to *99.50.

An egg and dart molding with double-looped dividers surmounted by a half-round and quasi hawk's beak profile forms the top of the frieze (Fig. 74). The color scheme is black and white; the uppermost, plain molding was black, the half-round white, and the eggs white, while the dividers and darts were black (cf. *ATK*, pl. 48:1, 2, 3, esp. no. 1 = *Sardis* X [1926] fig. 9 and pl. VII).

37 *Fig. 75.* NOEX 72.5. Upper right corner of egg and dart molding.

W. 0.16; H. 0.12; Th. 0.032, of background 0.022.
Ca. W230/S1100, near Sardis Expedition house.

Flat taenia above an egg and dart molding with the
darts at the top; below, a plain abacus (half-round
molding) and a flat area (cf. *ATK,* pl. 48:1). Hardly any
paint remains on the top surface but some can be
found within the details of the relief. We can therefore
restore the taenia and the abacus as red, the overall
background, centers of the eggs, and the darts as
white, and the relief borders of the eggs as black. We
cannot be sure whether the taenia was in fact painted
with chevrons since there is no evidence other than the
few specks of red; the same sort of reasoning applies
for the flat band at the bottom of the fragment—a few
specks of white are extended to cover the whole surface.

38 *Fig. 76.* T60.8:2399. Egg and dart above astragal.
   Archaic.
H. 0.113; W. 0.11; Th. 0.05.
AcN N1-5/E10-15 Byzantine fill.

The piece is much battered, especially at the upper
right, so that the upper plain band must be restored
largely by inference. Two eggs remain more or less intact and there are indications of a third to the right. Of
the astragal, two beads, the intervening reel, and half a
reel on the left survive. Below these is an irregular
break which allows just a small fragment of the background of the frieze to be made out.
   The paint has almost completely worn off except for
traces of black and white in the divisions. It is impossible to say whether the white is exclusively from the
undercoat or whether it may in some cases be from the
final scheme.
   For this combination of patterns and similar plastic
modeling, cf. a piece from Sardis now in the Istanbul
Museum (*ATK,* 72, no. 11, pl. 42).

39 *Fig. 77.* T60.16:2584. Egg and dart molding. After
   525.
H. 0.056; W. 0.08; Th. 0.027.
HoB ca. E0-5/S100-105 upper mixed fill near surface.

Top edge of frieze with rectangular molding above,
and egg and dart below in relief. A fragment of what
may have been a half-round molding probably divided
the upper portion from the lower, which is now lost.
That could well have been lotus buds or heraldic ani-

mals or a yet more elaborate scene. This piece has
rather crisp, fussy modeling which suggests that it is
late. If indeed it is, we should restore a much plainer
arrangement below.

40 *Fig. 78.* T64.33:6368. Egg and dart molding. 4th C.?
H. 0.05; W. 0.07; Th. 0.035.
PN W237-246/S348-353 *88.10.

Part of a small, simplified lotus flower is surmounted
by an egg and dart molding over which a plain strip, of
rectangular section, formed the original upper edge.
The egg and dart strip is set on a step slightly raised
above the level of the background for the lotus. The
elements of the molding are rather small (ca. 0.013)
and sharply differentiated, seeming to stand on their
own as discrete parts rather than being embellishments
for a continuous three dimensional band. This ten-
dency and the simplification of the lotus associates the
piece with the later types of the antefixes (see **91** for
discussion).

41 *Figs. 79–82.* T58.22:762. Spouted sima.
L. 0.15; W. 0.092, with spout 0.095; H. 0.09.
BS W 1.

Most of the right half of a spouted sima. The corner
is preserved although much of the paint and a large
chip from the underside have been lost. There are considerable remains of the right side of the spout, although some of the transitional clay at the extreme
right has fallen off because of poor workmanship in
joining. The front face consists of a flat band ca. 0.06 in
width, which is decorated with an oblique black line
which comes from under the spout and terminates in a
tendril-like spiral (Fig. 79). At about half height there
is a blob of red paint. A plain half-round molding com-
pletes the face; this is decorated in alternating rectangles of white and red framed in black and divided by
thin white lines. The upper part of the spout is painted
in an oblique lattice pattern in black with small red
triangles. We might suppose that the height was about
0.16 by analogy with **31**, which is slightly larger in all
dimensions.
   The underside (Fig. 80) is painted in long tongues of
alternating red and black; they are divided by a white
border which in turn is divided between and around
the tongues by a thin black line. The painting on the
underside is very deep, extending back at least 0.09
m., which indicates considerable projection over the

edge of the roof (cf. **66** black and white diamonds; similar part of corner).

The absence of relief and the painting of the tongues make this piece one of the closest to mainland and West Greek terracottas that we have at Sardis. This similarity, however, does not extend to the color; for the red is distinctly Lydian and quite different from Corinthian red.

A number of constructional features are obvious at the broken edges of this piece, which reinforce our opinions about the handling of the actual clay: *1*. At the right side of the spout and the vertical face of the tile there is no paint and the surface has been roughened as if with a modeling tool or a piece of stick (Fig. 81). One may infer from this that there was a large triangular transitional piece which was carelessly attached. *2*. Where the bottom surface breaks away, under the spout and to its right (Fig. 82), there is a large hole and a smooth curving line against the face and bottom. This shows clearly that a round reinforcing roll was stuck in the inside corner but not enough care was taken to ensure that all the air bubbles were removed; consequently the piece was weakened and the bottom broke off.

42 *Fig. 83*. T67.12:7440. Star and scroll pattern. Ca. 575.
H. 0.19; W. 0.55; Th. 0.04.
PN W257-259/S327-334 *86.5 and W260-262.5/S325-327 *86.2.

Six joining fragments found close to one another were recomposed to form a substantially complete star and scroll sima. The width is that of the original as is the height. Sufficient parts of the design remain for the missing parts to be reconstructed with confidence.

Several pieces of this kind were found by Shear; the patterns agree exactly but the dimensions and surface preservation vary. Sima tiles with identical designs were found in the excavations at Gordion.

The basic components of this design are four rectangular panels alternating between the star element and the scroll element. Shear has described the type as well as I could hope to (*Sardis* X [1926] 32).

In the centre of the star type is a rounded boss, about which is a design with four equal bars and concave sides. From the end of each bar five plumes extend like the plumes of a palmette, between which, in the concavity of the design, are four rays or buds with slender points reaching to the corners of the panel. The relief of the design is highest at the base of the rays . . . On the adjoining panel a scroll pattern is represented which consists of two graceful S-shaped curves.

The curve on the right is arranged in a reversed position to the other, and is joined to it by narrow bands at the top and the bottom. Above the top band is a small bud-shaped ornament, and below it one small and three larger buds. Objects of similar shape appear above and below the lower band also, as well as on either side of the lower curve of the scroll, seeming here to spring from the side walls of the panel. The slender curving terminals of the scroll are finished by four rounded buttons.

The date of this piece is fixed by the stratigraphical context. It was found at the corner of a building on an exterior, cobbled floor. On this floor amidst a considerable amount of domestic debris we found a number of imported sherds, none of which could have been made after 550. Most noteworthy of these was a broken plastic vase in the form of a paunched hare (P67.78:7464) and a piece of a Corinthian aryballos with incised tongues (P67.140:7578; Figs. 84–85). Additional force for this conclusion comes from the close association of this area with the Altar of Cybele and gold refining area whose latest phase must be somewhat before 550 on the basis of sculptural and ceramic evidence. This is in direct contradiction to Åkerström's opinion (*ATK*, 84, 243) that the original use of this type was 550 or later. His view is based on style and what he feels appropriate for an ill-documented series of decorative reliefs, whereas our opinion is firmly set in the excavation levels, in conjunction with pottery of several styles.

Published: *BASOR* 191, 13; chronology discussed in "The Dating of Lydian Architectural Terracottas," paper by the author given to the annual meeting of the Archaeological Institute of America, see "Summaries of the Papers Presented," Seventy-Seventh General Meeting, Washington, D.C., Dec. 28–30, 1975, p. 6. For pieces found by Shear see *Sardis* X (1926) figs. 18–20, pl. XI; *ATK*, 75ff., 91, nos. 4–9, pls. 44ff., also p. 86, where the heights of the sima series are discussed. For tiles from Gordion see A. and G. Körte, *JdI* Ergänzungsheft 5 (1904) and *ATK*, 136–161, pls. 69–86. The Corinthian pottery is to be published by J. S. Schaeffer in a forthcoming Sardis volume.

43 *Frontispiece and Fig. 86*. T60.2:2289. MANISA. Scroll part of star and scroll. Ca. 540.
H. 0.16; W. 0.18; Th. 0.035.
PC ca. W235/S602 *90.50.

Two joining pieces from the scroll pattern of a star and scroll sima make up almost a whole panel with well preserved paint. The volutes and petals are painted black over a white ground; the end "buttons" of the scroll are red and the vertical border is red. Above the volutes is a horizontal border of chevrons in relief to right, alternating black and red, as in **44**; the background is white.

This piece uses some of the thickest slip I have encountered among the terracottas at Sardis. The left edge seems to have been adjusted by chipping after firing rather than having been cleanly cut while the clay was green. The back of the piece is covered with a cream slip.

Published: *BASOR* 162, 21, fig. 8.

44 *Fig. 87.* T61.11:3209. Scroll fragment. Last quarter 6th C.
H. 0.091; W. 0.108; Th. 0.033.
HoB W7/S99 *99.65.

This is the upper portion of a star and scroll sima showing the join between two panels. On the right are traces of the tip of the star; on the left much of the upper right hand volute of the scroll. The volute was painted in black, the background in white, upper border has black and white herringbone design pointing to left. The very top and back is painted with a red wash.

45 *Fig. 88.* T61.18:3285. Scroll fragment. Last quarter 6th C.
H. 0.125; W. 0.146; Th. 0.034.
HoB W9/S99 *99.60.

A three-petaled palmette springs from the upper junction of the volutes in a scroll pattern. Above that is set a maeander border in relief. The inner designs on this piece are on a much larger scale than is usual for our sima tiles. It may well have come from a decorative plaque with another function (cf. *ATK*, 72, no. 12, pl. 43:1).

46 *Fig. 89.* T61.60:3590. Scroll fragment. Late archaic.
H. 0.044; W. 0.061; Th. of background 0.015, of border 0.034.
PN S375/W245 *87.92-87.35.

This is the lowest part of the left hand curving volute of the scroll panel of a star and scroll sima. The scroll itself is painted black on a white background and has an additional fine black line to reinforce the shape. The bud or petal growing downward out of the union be-

tween the scrolls is white and outlined in black. The lower border is of alternating black and white rectangles. Underneath, black dots on a white background formed the pattern. This piece seems to represent an unparalleled way of coloring what is a well known and standard pattern.

47 *Fig. 90.* T61.77:3768. Star fragment. Late archaic.
H. 0.10; W. 0.098; Th. 0.034.
AcT ca. W25/N7 ca. *401.50-401.40.

This five-petaled palmette forms the extremity of the cross-like shape in the center of the star pattern. The palmette and cross were picked out in black paint, as was the central boss, of which about a quarter can be seen. It seems more likely that this is one of the horizontal members, but it is unclear whether it should be restored to left or to right.

48 *Fig. 91.* T63.60:5814. Scroll fragment. Late archaic.
H. 0.11; W. 0.07; Th. 0.024.
HoB W2-10/S117-122 *101.00-100.20.

This is the top portion of the left hand scroll in a panel much like **43**. The scroll is painted black and the petals red. What was presumably a white background has worn off, leaving only the body of the clay.

49 *Fig. 92.* T63.62:5870. Star fragment. Late archaic.
H. 0.095; W. 0.10; Th. 0.03.
Syn S5/E85 surface.

This is the central part of the star design. The raised boss in the middle is preserved as is most of the cross-like form which surrounds it and the rounded portions of the ends of two rays. Because all four edges are broken and this design is symmetrical, both vertically and horizontally, it is impossible to know which part is the top.

50 *Fig. 93.* T64.28:6355. Star and scroll fragment.
H. 0.14; W. 0.12; Th. 0.022.
Syn E126.75-128.00/S5-6 *96.50-96.00.

This piece is much battered but shows part of both the scroll pattern and the star. The lower right volute of the scroll can be made out and the left horizontal palmette of the star. The division between the panels can be seen but it is much abraded. Hardly any paint is preserved other than the white of the background.

51 *Fig. 94.* T61.45:3483. Lotus and bud frieze. Later 6th C.
H.0.11; W. 0.11; Th. 0.025.
PN W248.50/S372.70 ca. *88.00.

This is the upper band of a design probably comprised of two decorative bands in relief with a plain band between them. The largest element in this case is a continuous strip where lotus flowers and buds are depicted. This is unusual since the common arrangement is of lotus and palmette (*Sardis* X [1926] pl. XIII, upper register). Above the floral strip is a band of small triangles in relief. Nowhere are there traces of color but this does not seem to have been standard in this series.

52 *Fig. 94.* T63.27:5202. Lotus and bud frieze. 6th C.
H. 0.06; W. 0.098; Th. 0.022.
HoB E5-19/S115 *99.10.

Two joining fragments together make up part of the upper band of a two-register sima tile, as in **51**. The subject is the same and the scale similar; what differs in this piece is that the molded designs were painted red, and red paint was used also in the lower part to bring out the joining tendrils which were not strongly indicated in relief. Above the floral design is a band of small triangles in relief; they were also painted red. The background was white. A curious feature of this piece is that it has been broken obliquely through the bud, which is in the center. This has caused the bud to break off at the edges and suggests that some parts of the relief designs may have been done with appliqué pieces of clay from much smaller molds, after the fashion of some Hellenistic relief ware and Arretine pottery.

53 *Fig. 94.* T63.47:5451. Lotus fragment. 6th C.
H. 0.063; W. 0.09; Th. 0.023.
PN W233-235/S349-350 *88.20.

Practically all of one lotus blossom is preserved (the top of the right hand tip of the flower is broken away) and there are traces of a bud on each side. The left bud is only a trace, whereas the body of the right is substantially preserved. Above the flowers there is a row of small triangles, now much worn and lost entirely to the right of center. Below the buds is a painted red band tying them together and acting as a tendril. There are traces of red paint on the flowers too; the background used to be white. This is almost exactly the same as **52** and probably derived from the same mold.

54 *Fig. 94.* T64.40:6393. Lotus and buds. 6th C.
H. 0.072; W. 0.11; Th. 0.025.
PN W237-247/S347-354 *88.60.

A single lotus flower is flanked by two buds. Above them is a narrow border of triangles in relief. Below, the connecting tendrils are much worn although they do seem to have been originally in relief. Both the top and bottom edges appear to be original—certainly the lower edge is very straight. If the original height is preserved, the piece cannot have been part of a typical architectural terracotta but must come from a ceramic box or other small-scale decorative piece. I have included it, nevertheless, because of its close correspondences with **51** through **53**, which were undoubtedly from taller pieces.

55 *Fig. 94.* T64.30:6362. Lotus bud and flowers.
H. 0.065; W. 0.085; Th. 0.02.
PN W236-248/S349-353 *88.60-88.10.

The subject and scale are the same as the preceding. There is, however, a significant difference in the fact that the joining tendrils below the flowers are preserved in relief.

56 *Fig. 95.* NOEX 65.1. Lotus and palmette.
H. 0.103; W. 0.085; Th. 0.034.
Well, about 20 m. N of expedition compound (W250/S1100).

Top left corner piece of a lotus and palmette frieze from what must have been a double frieze with a flat division between the two zones (*Sardis* X [1926] pl. XII; *ATK*, pls. 46, 47). The tip of the lotus is black and the center red; the palmette has five leaves, three red and two black, growing from a red button; the loops connecting the lotuses and palmettes are black. The upper taenia is red and so is the top surface.

The left edge seems original; this is confirmed when one sees that it is usual to join the lotuses in this way rather than splitting them exactly down the middle. **57** has the same design on a slightly smaller scale.

57 *Fig. 95.* T62.31:4599. Lotus and palmette fragment. 6th C.
H. 0.125; W. 0.09; Th. 0.03.
PN/E testpit W, ca. W221/S381 *87.8.

Almost the whole of one lotus is preserved and one leaf of the left palmette. The pattern is set between two narrow moldings, the upper rectangular and the lower half round. Below that is a raised portion with irregular edges and of no particular shape. It is probably part of the bridging portion of the opening for the spout (cf. similar feature clearly visible *ATK*, pls. 46:1, 2; 47:1). There is no paint preserved.

58 *Fig. 95.* T62.12:4388. Lotus and palmette. Mid-6th C.
H. 0.68; W. 0.145; Th. 0.03 (with border).
TU, upper room fill (Fig. 2, No. 21). For description of TU see *BASOR* 170, 35f.

This design was hitherto unknown at Sardis in terracottas—unusual in that the lotus is in the form of a bud. Furthermore, the dimple in the middle seems strange when compared to the other flowers (**51–57**). The plants seem to be dependent but this is not certain. The upper border had a pattern of black and white chevrons pointing to right; the main field was white and the floral elements painted red and black.

59 *Fig. 96.* T61.89:3886. Maeander fragment. Mid-6th C.
H. 0.057; W. 0.062; Th. 0.021.
HoB W3-5/S89-90 *100.00-99.85.

Small fragment with a raised maeander pattern in black with white background. This pattern is very similar in its details to that of **27**.

60 *Fig. 96.* T63.23:5170. Maeander fragment. Mid-6th C.
H. 0.055; W. 0.115; Th. 0.03.
HoB E5/S110-115 to *99.30 floor.

The fretting of the relief maeander pattern is very badly worn; much of it is abraded and only specks of paint remain. From these we can see that, as usual in the channels, there was a white background, but we also find an extra surface design of red and black stripes on the frets, which is too indistinct to be made out for certain.

61 *Fig. 96.* T65.5:6637. Maeander fragment. 1st half 6th C.
H. 0.054; W. 0.06; Th. 0.023.
PN W288/S326.5 *86.1.

Most of the paint has worn off the top surface of this design, but enough remains to show that this piece probably had the standard color scheme of black frets in relief on a white background. The height of the piece corresponds to the height of the maeander pattern. In spite of the undistinguished appearance of this piece, it may have some importance for the dating of the type, since pieces found in this context can be securely placed in the middle of the sixth century or, if anything, earlier.

62 *Fig. 96.* T65.11:6740. Maeander (perhaps with sphinx's tail).
H. 0.095; W. 0.07; Th. 0.025, of background 0.015.
PN W281/S322 *86.3.

A maeander in relief over an almost semicircular coil pattern ending in a button-like knob. In the center is a dot in relief. The overall color scheme is black for the designs in relief and white for the backgrounds.

This is a puzzling piece; at first sight it seems to be a fragment from a star and scroll, but if one examines the overall design closely, there appears to be no section that corresponds to the pattern of our piece. One difficulty arises from the fact that the "button" is finished on its sides and broken at the bottom, so that the relief coil must have continued, but there is no provision for linking it to the side of another coil. Usually the button extends slightly beyond the edges of both scrolls. An additional deviation from the star and scroll design is the maeander border, since it is not found on any standard examples of this pattern; even allowing for some other variety, the coil on our fragment is still too far away from the border. Another suggestion which I favor, although it is essentially speculative, is that we have part of the tail of a walking sphinx or griffin. The dot in the center would then be the tip of the tail and the button the caudal swell found in some felines. The objection to this, however, is that the representations we have, both on terracottas and on East Greek pottery, do not show the tail curling in on itself at the end. Nevertheless it would seem easier to find a new variety in the relatively uncommon realms of figurative simas than in the standard repetition of a well-worn type which does not admit much invention.

63 *Fig. 97.* T60.33:2895. Guilloche fragment. 1st half 6th C.
H. 0.78; W. 0.82; Th. 0.029.
HoB E5-10/S100 *99.80-99.60 floor.

This is a fragment of a guilloche border in relief with many-petaled rosettes in the loops between the cables.

The top edge, the front, and the back are finished; all other edges are broken. The ornament bears considerable resemblance to that of a lateral sima in Boston, whose findspot is unknown (*ATK*, 42, pl. 16:1). This has connections with Sardis for other reasons: it was acquired in Smyrna and its subject is reminiscent for Åkerström of a piece from Sardis in Istanbul, which he published for the first time (*ATK*, pl. 42), antithetical sphinxes pawing at a tree. Åkerström puts the Boston piece in the later sixth century. On stratigraphic grounds, our piece seems more likely to belong to the mid-sixth century or earlier. This design is also found in a form more like that of our fragment on a piece of unknown provenience in the Louvre which has been the subject of much argument (*Sardis* X [1926] 28ff. and *ATK*, 43f.).

64 *Fig. 97.* T61.57:3581. Guilloche fragment. 6th C.
H. 0.103; W. 0.10; Th. 0.02.
BE rooms N of BE-H and MC (ca. E17-20/S80-100) fill *98.00-97.00.

This piece is similar to the foregoing but there is no original edge at top or bottom. To make up for this inferiority, a greater expanse of white painted background for the main scene has been preserved, and traces of black are found on the underside of the left-hand cable of the guilloche.

65 *Fig. 98.* T62.39:4762. Zigzag border.
H. 0.064, of border 0.035; W. 0.076; Th. 0.04.
HoB W23.5/S99.5 *99.5.

Top rectangular molding of sima; part of top surface is painted red but back is merely smoothed. The front of the molding (taenia) is flat with a coarsely painted zigzag design in black over white. The whole design is bordered by a glossy red stripe sometimes streaked with black.

66 *Fig. 99.* T70.3:8093. Painted under-border. Ca. 550.
H. 0.07; W. 0.11; Th. 0.06.
PN W237/S346 *87.5.

This is the lower corner of a spouted sima tile exactly like that of **31**. While the structure is the same, the decoration is much more elaborate, and very like the projecting under-edge of **21** and **22**. The part with the design of black diamonds surrounded by narrow black stripes is about 0.07 m. wide and there is a broad

band of streaky reddish-black. This is preserved to a thickness of ca. 0.04 m. in this example. The soffit of **31** was painted also, but with a thin, though glossy, red paint. One assumes that this painting of the undersides was done for neatness in case some of the projecting tiles did not fit the spaces prepared for them as well as they should have.

67 *Figs. 100–101.* T65.18:6857. Reworked fragment. 6th C.
H. 0.133, of "turret" 0.045; W. 0.085; Th. 0.03.
Syn E89.00-87.5/N3.8-4.3 *92.6-91.6.

Although this piece is lacking in artistic appeal as a result of its poor preservation, it can be identified as having belonged to a series of simas normally decorated with large lotus flowers flanking a spout. These flowers are surmounted by a plain dark band and a row of "turrets" in relief, which take the form of rounded waves with very deep troughs between them (see Fig. 101). The color scheme is the usual one with the plain molding picked out in reddish-black and the main surface done in white. The turrets of the pieces illustrated in *Sardis* X (1926) have red spots in the upper center, but there is no trace of a spot here. Some traces of the black paint of the recessed background to the turret can still be seen. What makes our piece noteworthy is the fact that the background between the turrets has been carved away, giving one the feeling of free-standing openwork, even though only one turret is preserved.

For tiles from Sardis with similar turrets see *Sardis* X (1926) fig. 22, pls. XIII, XIV; *ATK*, 77. no. 22, pls. 49, 50.

Antefixes

The antefixes found by our excavations are all of the same type, that is trapezoidal and belonging to the Corinthian system of ceramic roof covering.[6] Normally the angle of the apex of an antefix and cover tile is ca. 130°; the sloping sides are often markedly concave. It is curious that there seem to be no fragments of decorated edges from eave tiles of the form suggested by the illustrations cited above, which is common in peninsular Greece. What we are calling antefixes are in fact the closed ends of the final cover

6. Cf. Orlandos I 85, fig. 57; Dinsmoor, 44, fig. 16; *ATK*, 196f., fig. 64, pl. 57:5.

tiles in the series running down the roof from the ridge. An excellent example of a plain cover tile of this type, which is open at both ends, is preserved in the Archaeological Museum, Istanbul (*ATK*, 36:1).

Since roofing systems using this arrangement are incompatible with systems using spouted simas (e.g. **31**), they probably belong to later buildings, as this arrangement of tiles becomes almost universal practice in the Greek world. It is possible that both methods of roofing may have been in use during the late archaic period, since the volutes of type 1 (below) look distinctly early and several examples were found in association with sixth century pottery.

A feature of the antefix designs at Sardis is that almost all of them stem from one idea: a palmette between two volutes. This can take a number of forms, such as two separate volutes back to back, looking rather like snails, with a palmette sprouting from the space between (see **68** Fig. 103) or a very simplified "tree between scrolls," which has very little surface resemblance to its predecessors (see **81** Fig. 109).

I have distinguished three main types for the antefixes collected by the Harvard-Cornell Expedition and subgroups in both type 1 and type 2 (Fig. 102). I have ignored the question of the direction of the spirals since this seems to be more a practical matter in the workshop, when one is dealing with molds or casts, than an important question of design, but there are certainly instances of reversed spirals, which some might consider as yet another subvariety. Another type (4) is added which has not been identified among the finds of the recent excavations but is illustrated and described by Åkerström, as found during Butler's campaigns (*ATK*, 70, no. 4, now in New York). Set out below are the chief characteristics of the types.

Type 1 Floral palmette between two plastic snail-like volutes.
    a. Horizontal, finished, rounded ends to volutes.
    b. Vertical, cut-off ends to volutes.
Type 2 *a.* Tree-like palmette flanked by horizontal double scrolls.
    b. Similar to *a* but with a smaller palmette growing directly upwards and out of the scroll as it changes direction.
Type 3 A much simplified version of 2 in which the tree-like palmette hardly varies in width from stalk to leaf and the double scroll is simplified and reduced to an open double ended hook (**91** Fig. 117).
Type 4 Tree-like form between heraldically opposed animals.

Throughout the series of antefixes there is evidence of what may fairly be called shoddy workmanship. Pieces of clay can be seen to have been pushed together into a form or mold when they were too dry to make a close bond. This can be discerned from the stress and breakage lines, together with the presence of air bubbles. The problem can be seen on contemporary and earlier pottery, especially the hydriae, whose breakage patterns (at shoulder and foot) often reveal lack of attention to sufficient dampness for joining and reinforcing the different parts of large vases. There is no sign that the faces of the antefixes were colored in anything other than a light red slip or wash, which normally corresponds approximately to Munsell soil color numbers 2.5YR5/8-6/8; he calls it "light red"—traditionally "brick red" or "terracotta"!

Type 1

68 *Fig. 103*. T65.10:6722. Palmette and single volute. Late 6th C.
W. 0.125; H. 0.085; P.L. 0.145.
PN W280-285/S320-325 *87.2-86.7.

An almost complete example of the front face, missing only a small piece at the right side. The palmette spreads at both top and bottom and is flanked by volutes with the ends pointing to the outside corner. A small palmette sprouts from the angle of the volute and the whole design is framed in relief. The stratigraphy suggests a late sixth or fifth century date.

69 *Fig. 104*. T61.107:4086.
H. 0.071; W. 0.06; Th. 0.043; wall of tile 0.015.
HoB W4/S86 *99.00.

As foregoing. Right-hand volute and edge of palmette. Most of the outer frame is still preserved. Well modeled. Clay body is rather gritty.

70 *Fig. 104*. T62.14:4390.
H. 0.045; W. 0.103; Th. 0.045.
HoB W25/S90 *99.90.

Gable and upper left side with volute growing upwards. Two leaves of central palmette remain and three of left palmette. Narrow border on upper edge.

71 *Fig. 104.* T64.32:6367.
H. 0.06; W. 0.09; Th. 0.015.
PN W237-246/S348-353 *88.10.

Right volute and palmette. The upper right corner is the only original edge.

Type 2a

72 *Fig. 105.* T64.10:6013.
H. 0.68; W. 0.145; Th. 0.035.
PN W255-259/S344-350 *88.2-87.95.

Almost complete face, lacking right edge; wide-spreading palmette flanked by tightly curled double scrolls.

73 *Fig. 105.* T64.7:5989. 4th C.?
H. 0.08; W. 0.053; Th. 0.05.
PN W276-277/S342-346 *87.90-87.70.

Left half and some of upper right preserved. Dating based on stratigraphy.

74 *Fig. 105.* T63.37:5284.
H. 0.08; W. 0.09; Th. 0.031.
PN W224/S340.50 *88.40.

Peak of gable with well preserved palmette.

75 *Fig. 106.* T61.68:3651.
H. 0.076; W. 0.12; Th. 0.03.
HoB E5/S95 *99.70-99.50.

Complete but very battered antefix with only the inside spirals of the pairs showing; most likely a five-leaved palmette but not very clear, cf. **79**.

76 *Fig. 107.* T63.52:5605.
H. 0.07; W. 0.07; Th. 0.07.
PN W29/S245 to *86.7.

Almost complete double scroll; right portion of the design would be beyond the edge. Above the scroll is an isolated oval blob, apparently not part of the central palmette.

77 *Fig. 107.* T64.43:6499.
H. 0.075; W. 0.086; Th. 0.052.
PN W239/S352.5-353 *87.70.

Same type as foregoing; slightly more than half of a complete face is preserved including the central palmette. As in **64**, the right part of the scroll would go beyond the edge and there is a blob above it.

78 *Fig. 108.* T60.37:2923.
H. 0.085; W. 0.14; L. 0.125.
AcT trench E pit M, A-B/3-4 ca. *99.15.

Almost complete but surface is abraded.

79 *Fig. 107.* T60.9:2412.
H. 0.073; W. 0.09; Th. 0.03.
PC ca. W240-245/S600-605 *88.24-88.

Crisply modeled but simplified palmette.

80 *not ill.* T72.1:8192. 4th C.?
H. 0.072; W. 0.072; Th. 0.018.
AT trench 2, W115-117/S1226-1231 *98.73.

As foregoing; complete right half of front face. The upper part of the frame is carelessly finished and the surface much abraded.

Published: *Sardis* R1 (1975) 85, fig. 176.

81 *Fig. 109.* NOEX 71.17.
W. 0.132; H. 0.08; Th. 0.003.
From vineyard below Butler's house
(ca. W0-100/S1100-1200).

As foregoing; about three-quarters of an antefix with scrolls flanking a five-leaved palmette on a stem.

Type 2b

82 *Fig. 110.* T64.15:6065.
H. 0.07; W. 0.093; Th. 0.03.
PN W258-262/S338-339 below *88.5.

Almost all of left face preserved. Design is a sub-variety of type 2 in that the scroll is uneven and a long three-branched palmette grows outwards from the upper angle between the spirals.

83 *Fig. 111*. T64.44:6514.
H. 0.08; W. 0.98; Th. 0.02.
PN W239/S353 *85.85-83.85.

Design same as foregoing but right half is preserved and whole stem of vertical palmette.

84 *not ill*. T61.63:3600.
H. 0.04; W. 0.065; Th. 0.04.
HoB stone circle E5/S95 *99.60.

As foregoing; edge of left-hand scroll is showing.

85 *not ill*. T61.64a:3619.
H. 0.08; L. 0.10; Th. 0.076.
HoB wall W of hearth E5/S100 *99.60-99.10.

As foregoing; top of gable preserved.

86 *Fig. 112*. T60.29:2878.
H. 0.057; W. 0.128; L. 0.175.
PN room B, ca. W255/S375 *89.00-88.50.

As foregoing; simplified palmette growing upwards from scroll.

87 *Fig. 113*. T62.22:4457.
H. 0.08; W. 0.12; Th. 0.08.
PN, Street of Pipes W243/S380 *88.7

Much the same as foregoing but almost all of the design has flaked off except for lower part of the scroll at the extreme right.

88 *Fig. 114*. T63.26:5201. 3rd C.
Size is irregular: 0.06 by 0.07.
HoB E0/S115, to *80.80, from a well.

Inner spiral of right side and much simplified palmette above and beside it. The only finished edge is that of the right gable. Buff wash on exterior, slightly browner than body.

89 *Fig. 115*. T62.28:4550.
W. 0.12; H. 0.08; L. 0.10.
PN near W235/S377 *89.20 Roman fill.

Gable, central palmette, and upper parts of inner scrolls preserved.

90 *Fig. 116*. T68.19:7854.
W. 0.09; H. 0.07.
PN W293/S325, to Antiochus III destruction ca. *86.00.

Most of left (double) scroll preserved; there are original edges on three sides. The spiral at left is much the larger. A singular feature of this example is that, instead of the usual three-leaved palmette, there are two stiff stalks with bulbous ends sprouting from the upper angle of the scroll.

Type 3

91 *Fig. 117*. T63.24A:5194. 4th C.?
W. 0.133; H. 0.075; L. 0.07
HoB E0/S115 to *87.47.

This is the best preserved of several antefixes found together in a well (**92–94**). The face is almost all preserved and the design represents a shift towards coarser modeling and simplified elements in the design. The central palmette has three leaves only and the outer two have a pronounced droop. The stem of the central palmette has gained a small oval bar set at half height and the scrolls are not only almost reduced to mere hooks but are set obliquely, pointing towards the central palmette and the gable. The three-leaved palmette at the angle of the scroll is now a single pointed lobe directed into the "eaves." A portion of the bottom edge is broken away.

92 *not ill*. T63.24B:5194.
W. of bottom edge 0.035; H. of r. edge 0.04.
Found with **91**.

Right side of design similar to foregoing.

93 *Fig. 117*. T63.24C:5194.
H. 0.07; W. 0.095; D. 0.052.
Found with **91**.

As foregoing, right side and most of central palmette preserved. Design on this piece at bottom of palmette confirms that there are two elements on the stem below the horizontal center piece, which had seemed a possibility on **77**. The whole thing has a very disjointed look, compared to the flowing organic appearance of earlier works.

94 *not ill.* T63.24D:5194.
Irregular shape: W. 0.04; H. 0.06; Th. 0.03.
Found with **91**.

As foregoing; left scroll and lobe; part of bottom edge preserved.

95 *Fig. 118.* T62.17:4424. Central palmette.
H. 0.085; W. 0.102; Th. at top 0.05.
HoB E0-5/S100-105 *99.50.

Central palmette preserved to its full height; the design is tree-like and formalized as in **91**. The left half of a spiral scroll remains at right; surface badly worn.

96 *Fig. 118.* T63.55:5742.
H. 0.075; W. 0.19; Th. 0.03.
HoB E0-W5/S115-117 *99.9-99.4.

Substantially the same pattern as **91** but much cruder design and finish. The upper leaves of the palmette stick out stiffly and do not swell or curl.

97 *not ill.* T69.8:8016. Central portion.
H. 0.78; W. 0.10; Th. 0.015.
PN W265-260/S320-325 above *86; unstratified tile fallen from scarp in NE corner of trench.

Much as **96** but surface much more worn; the cross piece on the palmette appears to link the spiral scrolls.

98 *not ill.* T61.67:3650.
H. 0.072; W. 0.12; D. 0.058.
HoB stone circle, S E5/S95 *99.7-99.5.

As **97** but more of gable preserved.

99 *Fig. 118.* T61.105:4049. Left scroll and central palmette.

H. 0.063; W. 0.079; D. 0.039.
HoB, S edge W10-15/S105 *100-99.6.

The palmette has become even more tree-like than that of our type-piece (**91**) but is quite indistinct as if the mold had been worn. The scrolls, too, seem to have longer proportions deriving from an even more offhand curling of the ends.

Disc Acroterion

100 *Figs. 119–122.* UNINVENTORIED 1965. Fragment of disc acroterion.
L. 0.19; H. 0.11; max. Th. 0.07; W. of tongues ca. 0.035; est. diam. ca. 0.80-1.00.
PN W293-296.5/S330-332 *86.55-86.4.

A cavetto moulding from the outer edge of the disc was made into tongues by painting and incised lines. These tongues are alternately black and red, divided by a vertical band of white on each side of an incised line; traces of paint are still in the incised line.

This piece is very close in design and dimensions to one from Larisa and to others from Bassae and Sparta. It is unusual not so much for its form (another in three fragments is described and illustrated in *ATK*, 83, fig. 26, now in the Metropolitan Museum of Art, New York), as for its color. Its color scheme does not follow that created by the heavy slip of the simas nor that of the streaked ware so popular in later Lydian ceramics of the archaic era, but approximates much more closely that of mainland pottery, in particular the purplish red and semi-opaque white of Corinthian and Corinthian-influenced wares.

If our piece follows the general structural arrangement indicated for the Larisa disc (*ATK*, pl. 21:3) the fragment would be properly located about three bands from the extreme edge, at the point where the back is reinforced to brace the acroterion on the roof, but the fragment as preserved seems closer to the piece from Sparta. There is a curious incised diamond pattern on the oblique face at the back of our piece. It is lightly indented and at present there is no paint remaining, but the indentations show up as shiny in raking light. It seems an illogical place for further structural additions; perhaps it is the remains of marking out the rear face in a diamond pattern which, after all, was a favorite design for the pantiles and cover tiles.

Published: *BASOR* 215, 56, fig. 25. For Larisa parallel see *Larisa* II pl. 68; *ATK*, pls. 20:1–2, 21:3; for Bassae, Van Buren, 182, no. 15, figs. 56–58; for Sparta, Koch, 94, no. 1, fig. 45.

Ridge Tile

101 *Fig. 123.* UNINVENTORIED 1963. Fragment of ridge tile.
L. 017; W. 0.17; Th. ca. 0.02; est. diam. 0.12; W. of flange 0.07.
HoB W15-20/S110-114 *100-99.7.

This seems to be part of a ridge tile of approximately cylindrical shape with a flange at one end. This part is grooved on the top surface but plain underneath. There is no trace of cutouts for descending rows of cover tiles but the size and shape of the piece preclude its being a cover tile. Some black paint is preserved in the grooves and the exterior is painted with a reddish wash. There are no internal indications to date this piece which is said to have been found while "removing Hellenistic pavement" in HoB (noted by excavator, G. F. Swift, Jr.). This in itself does not prevent its being considered older but the overall feeling of such decoration as remains is not in the archaic spirit, nor is the artistic technique that which we see in the painting of archaic pantiles and cover tiles.

Pantiles and Cover Tiles

As was the case for the simas, we must continue to rely on the finds from Butler's expedition to establish the dimensions of the tiles used for covering the general expanse of the roof, since the recent excavations have not produced any whole examples of pantiles or of cover tiles. Examples of these are given by Åkerström (*ATK,* 68), who reports measurements of 0.60 by 0.45 for a complete pantile and 0.64 by 0.19 for a complete cover tile. It would seem that an absolutely standard width for pantiles was not established since there is considerable variety of width among the complete spouted sima tiles, and one would suppose it necessary for the joins of the pantiles to correspond to those of the simas to avoid confusion and irregularity in the laying of the cover tiles.

As with the sima friezes, the pieces are often small, but one may, nevertheless, draw important conclusions from them and expand the idea of roof decoration to include the whole area and not merely the edges of the roof. Both pantiles and cover tiles were painted;

the overriding idea behind the design was to combine a series of diamond patterns and oblique lines into a vibrant, colorful scheme, using the same repertoire of color as for the molded sima tiles, though frequently with less careful preparation of the white undercoat. In the present state of the evidence it would be premature to insist upon any particular set scheme, and the beauty of the system is that it permits much variety of arrangement. One might compare the patterns on some barn roofs in the United States and those of the fortification walls of the medieval city of Ani, capital of Armenia, where complex patterns are built up from simple elements. In those examples, squares rather than diamonds are the fundamental unit but the lines of the design are made oblique by the device of progressively offsetting the squares one place in each row. Some possibilities of the Lydian system are indicated in the sketch, Figure 124.

Groups of pantiles, many of which were saved but not inventoried, help to give a picture of the overall covering of the roof and provide information on the fitting and setting of the tiles. For instance, one knows in an abstract way that the tiles hook onto one another on the underside—but how is it done? Is there a uniform system which does not change much, except in superficial details, over the centuries? The earlier, gaily decorated pantiles seem to have had a slight downward curve at what I take to be the lower end in order to hold the tile in the row below, which should have had a slight upward curve. Only one piece which has the upward curve has survived but others have been assumed. An apparently later series, with more explicit use of raised bars or turned over edges as locking devices, comes from a well, originally of Persian date, in which 233 fragments of tiles were found. In this group we can see how the upper and lower ends of the tiles were treated so that they would be locked in place on the building. Exactly the same method was used for locking the pantiles in position on the temple of Artemis at Ephesus, endowed by Croesus (Hogarth, *Ephesus,* Atlas pl. XI). A later solution along the same lines is found among a group of pieces from an area in HoB which is thought to be Hellenistic in general date, although pieces of earlier pottery and bronze were found there too (*BASOR* 166, 7ff.). In this design the down-turned lower edge is much heavier and the bar on the upper edge of the next row of tiles is much fatter; size and especially thickness seem to have been desirable features at this time.

There are several changes in pantile shape and decoration during the years we are considering. There is a movement towards more precise fitting of the interlocking members and away from the lively painting of the roof in different colors. Tiles are still painted but in plain colors, red or black, in the form of a wash, for white has disappeared and there are no more diamonds. My feeling is that the process of tile making was simplified; the desire for economy grew more intense and the elegant nonfunctional decorations were dispensed with. The modern world, where mass production in factories has squeezed out individual craftsmen, offers many analogies. This difference is not necessarily just a matter of individual economy but corresponds to the dramatic shifts in taste and style from the archaic and Orientalizing eras to the classical period, where elegance subsists in spare simplification rather than in rich elaboration.

The cover tiles follow much the same pattern of development, painted first in neat diamonds, later painted wholly in red or black, finally in an overall red wash, which has in many cases worn off. In terms of construction there is a change from flat-sided cover tiles to a shape where the sloping surface is concave (see **108** Fig. 129); this is mirrored in the shapes of the antefixes. The sagging may be explained in origin by the use of too plastic a clay and by removing the pieces from the molds before they were properly set; it could be that, at a later time, what had first occurred from carelessness was continued by design. This style of cover tile is the same as that used for the cover tiles of the Croesus temple at Ephesus (Hogarth, *Ephesus, Atlas* pl. XI). Most of these pieces do not have great intrinsic interest, but as groups, the members of which have slight differences but greater similarities, they give us considerable information which I have attempted to summarize above. In addition, a few of the more noteworthy or curious pieces are included in the catalogue to give the reader a feel for the nature of the information and its source, without attempting a lengthy list of every piece of pantile retrieved at Sardis. I have followed what seems to me the chronological order in each category, first pantiles, then cover tiles.

Pantiles

102 *Fig. 125*. T61.36:3424. Painted fragment. Mid-6th C.
W. 0.13; H. 0.075; Th. 0.02.
PN W265/S355 *87.4 floor and fill.

Part of a white painted tile which had a red and black streaked diamond in the center. No original angle of the diamond is preserved but that of the lowest point

can be calculated as about 47 to 50°. A tile with similar decoration, from Gordion, is described and illustrated by Åkerström (*ATK*, 147, pl. 81:1). Judging by the excavational context of this piece and its technique one should place it in the mid-sixth century.

103 *Fig. 125*. T60.39:2945.
W. 0.125; H. 0.10; Th. 0.02.
PN room B, drain (general area W248-259/S370-380) *87.6.

As foregoing but lower edge preserved; the white paint was applied after the dark as is shown by a dulling of the edges where there was overlapping. Once again the angle of the tip of the diamond was between 40 and 50°. The bottom has a ledge extending a little beyond the thickness of the piece.

104 *Fig. 125*. T60.18:2600. Upper portion.
W. 0.082; H. 0.089; Th. 0.017
AcT G-I/5-7 *103.2-102.6 fill.

No original edge but combination of the color scheme and the raised part indicate that this is very near the top edge and that the interlocking (mechanism) was accomplished by the simple turning up of the top edge in order to catch onto the downturned lip of the tile above (cf. **103**). This piece would have had a white diamond in contrast to **102**.

105 *Fig. 126*. T60.28:2839.
W. 0.423, of edge 0.02; H. 0.165, of edge and pan 0.045; Th. 0.025.
PN room C (general area W245-259/S365-372) *89.5-88.25.

Wide piece of pantile including some of the original edge. This particular piece was painted black overall with no sign of a diamond which suggests that it is not archaic although it is certainly Lydian.

Cover Tiles

106 *Fig. 127*. T61.106:4054.
H. 0.105; W. 0.085; Th. 0.025, 0.043 at point of gable.
HoB W4-5/S86 *99.40-98.90.

Piece of lower edge of cover tile. The point of a diamond motif in brownish black remains with a white background; the surface is poorly preserved. This diamond has an oblique angle at the lower corner suggesting that on a standard length cover tile the design was repeated. The front edge is also painted—red. The context and level at which this piece was found makes it one of our earliest pieces. It is certainly more massive than the other pieces. If it is a really early piece it could belong to a phase before the standardization of the diamond patterns.

107 *Fig. 128.* T61.16:3277.
W. 0.08; H. 0.11; Th. 0.014.
HoB E10/S90 (wall of round building) *99.40.

The tip of a white diamond on red ground. The ground was actually painted last as the picture shows.

Note that the point of the diamond design is 0.02 from the edge of the piece and this edge itself is not original. The angle of the apex is ca. 30°.

108 *Fig. 129.* T61.50:3531.
L. 0.31; P.W. 0.11; est. complete W. 0.14; H. 0.04.
PN W255/S370 fill to ca. *89.25.

A considerable portion of a cover tile with the gable and one edge preserved. The upper sides are quite concave; they and the vertical sides are painted with streaky red/black paint. The form of the tile corresponds to those published from the Croesan Artemisium at Ephesus (Hogarth, *Ephesus*, Atlas pl. XI).

III STYLE AND CHRONOLOGY

As can be seen from the catalogue and by comparison with collections from elsewhere, the excavations at Sardis have produced an outstanding variety of subjects for ornamental friezes. This variety strengthens our capacity to study this class of architectural revetment in terms of its depiction of figures, animal, human or patterned, although it requires imagination to bring the fragments to life, to add the missing pieces to the puzzle. To do this we have had to range widely in the search for comparative material; indeed I believe that there is great value in considering designs or technical methods from as broad a selection of arts as possible. This need is more or less forced upon us by the nature of the terracottas themselves. They are of baked clay and painted in the colors appropriate to pottery. In fact they share a close relationship in color and technique both of manufacture and of decoration with the more elegant class of Lydian pottery. This in turn is closely linked with the styles of East Greek pottery known under the general headings of Wild Goat Style and Fikellura, as is demonstrated by large numbers of real pieces and the local imitations found in HoB and PN. In addition, a spectacular find of large-scale pots painted in this technique at Northeast Wadi (No. 16, on plan Fig. 2; Fig. 130), not far from the Temple of Artemis, brings the approximation much closer, because the sizes of the animal figures (*Sardis* R1 [1975] 123, figs. 313–316) are very close to those on the terracottas.

The frame of presentation on our terracotta friezes is quite different from that on most kinds of the decorated pottery we draw upon for comparison, since terracottas of our type are bound to a rectangular frame allowing only two or three figures to be shown in close relationship. It is granted that there are examples of continuous relief friezes, for example at Larisa in Aeolis, Düver in southern Phrygia and Murlo in Etruria, but they are in fact repetitions of the same composition, producing a horizontal flow more through the absence of borders than from continued invention of the kind one finds on the treasury of the Siphnians at Delphi or the drums of the Croesan temple of Artemis at Ephesus. A closer analogy in stone might be, as has been pointed out before (*ATK* p. 19, 180, 234; Demangel 205ff.), the frieze and metopes of the facade of the temple of Athena at Assos. To consider the widest range of subjects in appropriate frames one must therefore look to metal objects in which relief decoration is employed and one immediately finds rich sources of comparanda for schemes of arrangement and for subject matter. Particularly close and apt are the single scenes, enframed by square decorative patterns, found on sheet metal tripod legs and shieldbands. The most accessible groups of this type of material are recent finds from Olympia and well known pieces from Etruscan tombs—these have been listed with the item in the catalogue or in the discussion on chronology if a close argument using particular pieces or groups is required.

Large-scale sculpture, especially work in relief, cannot be neglected because the best terracottas not only have bright paint and firm outlines but also have remarkably delicate modeling, and by drawing on the results of longer established study of these trends we can sometimes find help in fixing the chronological place of particular pieces. Especially noteworthy in this regard is the interconnection of the grave stelai from Samos, whose finial ornaments take the form of volutes, with ceramic designs of this kind in East Greek pottery and a finial for a marble stele found in the fields near Sardis (Fig. 131); these interconnections helped us to find a place for the luxuriant volutes and palmettes used on what seems to be the earliest type of Lydian antefix.[1]

This wide searching among different media, all having a close relationship with architectural terracotta decoration, is useful for deciding inconographical questions or different possibilities of design, but it has another important advantage, the possiblity of establishing chronological relationships between our pieces and outside objects and subsequently among the pieces themselves. The process is not new; it is a fundamental tool of most archaeological and art historical judgments. What is regarded as more questionable is the interlocking of the various media, all of which have their specialists and particular techniques. This of course only works for a piece which is carefully made and carries with it sufficient possiblities of linkage; thus we cannot say much about a piece which consists of a maeander pattern and a lion's paw (27) unless there is something peculiar about either of them. On the other hand a human head or part of the torso, for instance, says much more about the attitude of the creators or the forms which were regarded as standard for the time and place.

We are in a situation where circularity of argument is a real danger, but we hope that the large number of variables, which should cross-check, will help to minimize the risk. Another way of placing the pieces chronologically, which is particularly useful at Sardis, is through their stratigraphic context. Clearly, the full impact of this is not yet available, since the two sectors which produced the most terracottas and the most pottery (both Lydian and imported), HoB and PN, have not yet been fully analysed and published. Even so, two important facts have come to light. First, the use of the specific design known as the star and scroll pattern can be put about 25 years earlier than the most recent literature suggests (ATK, 84f. and 42). Second, Shear's original estimate of ca. 600 for the earliest terracottas, although denied in recent literature, has been confirmed by new finds.[2] He based his dating on the correspondence of a Lydian column krater found among the decorated tiles to Early Corinthian column

kraters. In our sector, Northeast Wadi, two very similar column kraters were found in 1969 (Fig. 132; *Sardis* R1 [1975] 122 f., figs. 299, 306–319 ff.) in close context with painted ware, both imported and local, which must be dated before 600 B.C. This does not require that all architectural terracottas be dated around 600 B.C., but it does restore credibility to the idea that these are essentially products of the Lydian Empire and that invention in types and subject was reasonably complete before the Persian conquest in 547 B.C. A parallel situation exists in the current opinion that the coin production of Croeseids continued for a while under Persian rule; the types and metallic composition were already established and the chief *desideratum* was continuity, especially if we take the story of Diodorus about the short-lived looting of the city at face value.[3]

This not only revises the possible dating of Lydian architectural terracottas but provides a factual basis for freeing students from the bonds of a close chronological scheme that many have felt to be too binding, and to require too late a production of works which seemed much earlier. Even if Sardis were not the arbiter of the international style in the seventh century, she accepted it eagerly and quickly.

Local inspiration from nearby Aeolis has been regarded as responsible for the fineness of Sardian terracottas, but although there is a close similarity in general terms between the terracotta material from Larisa on Hermus and that from Sardis, particular differences in types or individual pieces are very striking. The closest parallel I have found is between fragments of disc acroteria (**100** and *Larisa* II pl. 68 and *ATK*, pl. 20, 21), whose restored forms seem to be very close in both scale and decoration. The nature of the material differs widely between Larisa and Sardis in that most of the pieces from Larisa come from the same place and were found at the same time (*Larisa* II 15–17). By contrast, the pieces from the new excavations at Sardis (1958–1974) have come in over the years from the different sectors as the excavations progressed, and some of them are classified as unexcavated or unstratified surface finds. Thus, in dealing with most of our material, we cannot even make the assumption

1. For discussion see *ATK*, 58; D. Kurtz and J. Boardman, *Greek Burial Customs* (London 1971) fig. 13, pls. 48, 49. G. M. A. Hanfmann, "On Lydian and Eastern Greek Anthemion Stelai," *RA* 1 (1976) 35–44, figs. 1–11.

2. *Sardis* X (1926) 4ff.; *contra* Åkerström, *ATK*, 84f., on stylistic grounds.

3. From Diodorus Siculus 9.33.4: "When Croesus had been taken prisoner and the pyre had been put out, and he saw that the city was being ravaged and much silver and gold as well as other things were being removed, he asked Cyrus what the soldiers were doing. With a laugh he replied that they were plundering Croesus' wealth. 'By Zeus, no,' said Croesus, 'it is yours they pillage: for Croesus no longer possesses a thing.' Cyrus was impressed by this argument and immediately changed his plans, checking the plundering of his soldiers and taking the belongings of the Sardians for the Imperial Treasury" (*Sardis* M2 [1972] no. 140).

that we are dealing with the roof decoration of a limited number of buildings, while at Larisa it is plausibly maintained that the majority of the terracottas came from early buildings close by the small temple on the acropolis (*Larisa* II 16 and fig. 2). There is, however, value in the fact that many of our pieces were retrieved in the ordinary course of the excavations and their interpretation and dating are dependent upon the context in which they were found.

Besides this variety of well authenticated historical contexts we have many subjects for the friezes, especially of animals, used as single or paired entities in a heraldic way. This, too, is in contrast to the mass of material from Larisa where, although there is a great variety of participants, each figure is used to make up a rich pictorial composition set in a frame. Much of the interpretation for this aspect of the excavations at Sardis must depend on the much better-preserved examples published by T. L. Shear (*Sardis* X [1926] passim), where a considerable number of pieces found at one place is illustrated. There is, unfortunately, no similarity to the Larisa find, since the pieces at Sardis were reused to form a tile grave in the Necropolis area, where no dependable traces of archaic building were discovered. The actual spot, known as the Lydian Terrace (ibid., fig. 1), has now been utterly removed by a bulldozer while making a road over the mountains to Ödemiş in the Cayster Valley, although one or two minor decorative pieces were recovered from the surface in the course of evening rambles near the spot before the road was built. We are obliged to depend heavily upon Shear's publication for the reconstruction and overall dimensions of complete pieces, because several of the examples recorded by him have been dispersed or lost in the course of wars and political uncertainty during the period from 1914 to 1923, between the outbreak of the First World War and the creation of an independent government in Ankara by Mustafa Kemal Atatürk. Some pieces survive in the Istanbul Archaeological Museum, and there are examples in the Metropolitan Museum of Art, New York, and in The Art Museum, Princeton University with which most of the principal excavators of what we call the first Sardis expedition were associated (see *ATK*, 96 for list of terracottas). The pieces in Princeton are generally small fragments, especially of antefixes and cover tiles, but the Metropolitan has some larger pieces which correspond to pieces figured by Butler (*Sardis* I [1922] figs. 72, 73, 74 r.) or Shear. The sizes of the recent finds, while corresponding to those in *Sardis* X (1926), where we have a high proportion of simas preserved, are much smaller than those ob-

served in other places (for example, Gordion) and this leads to the conclusion not only that we are dealing with much smaller buildings but that the architectural terracottas at Sardis were used for the adornment of private buildings as well.

This is clearly shown to have been the case in Etruria, where plain tiles and tiles decorated in relief were found together at the site of Acquarossa near Viterbo. They not only were together but lay as they had collapsed on the buildings which are typical houses at the site (Östenberg, 28). The terracottas from Acquarossa, those from Murlo,[4] and, indeed, archaic Etruscan architectural terracottas in general show great similarity of form and design to the whole range of architectural terracottas from many places in Asia Minor (see *ATK*, 269f.). Since an important feature of the pieces from both cultures is the use of a figured frieze in relief, which is the traditional decoration and protection for structures of the Ionic order (or those associated with that tradition), we must wonder whether direct Ionic influence does not precede Corinthian in the art of building and decorating in terracotta. This conclusion stems from the fact that Corinth, while noted for its art and ceramic work, is closely associated with Doric architecture and has no tradition of architectural terracottas decorated with figures in relief.

By giving for the first time a general account of the Lydian buildings and their decorative architectural terracottas, we hope to have presented material useful both for the study of house building in Asia Minor in the seventh and sixth centuries B.C. and for the study of the terracottas themselves. We have seen that the houses were small and simple, the materials plain. We have seen, too, a remarkable variety of decorative themes on the terracotta revetments. Color is there, with a striking use of the contrasts between black, white, brown, and orange-red. Texture we find too, in that this decorative art is sculptural; figures are molded in relief and so are the running patterns of the borders—egg and dart or maeander. Once again what we have discovered shows the deep penetration and acceptance of Greek styles, but equally we can see the deep-rooted attachment throughout Asia Minor (Greek cities included) to figures arranged in opposed pairs. By stressing the contexts in which our excavated pieces were found, we have shown that Lydian borrowings in the field of art occurred very soon after

---

4. Kyle Phillips, *AJA* 76 (1972) 249ff.; G. Colonna and C. E. Östenberg, eds., *Gli Etruschi, Nuove Ricerche e Scoperte* (Viterbo 1972).

their first appearance in the centers of Greek invention: Corinth, Sparta, Athens, Ephesus, and Larisa. From all these places, in politics and in art, the Lydians learned something, and our work has hinted at it although we have few opportunities to appreciate it in the Lydian terracottas in their complete state.

For chronology, too, I believe this study has helped lay the groundwork for further firmly based studies of the medium in inner Anatolia. Truly my scheme—that the figured pieces are largely products of the Lydian Empire—is in conflict with current views, but it is an opinion which was once commonplace and is now supported by fresh evidence derived from the most trustworthy source available: the stratigraphic sequence.

CONCORDANCE

Inventory Number	Catalogue Number	Figure Number
T63.37:5284	74	105
T63.42:5379	15	47
T63.47:5451	53	94
T63.49:5572	1	30, 31, 32
T63.52:5605	76	107
T63.55:5742	96	118
T63.60:5814	48	91
T63.61:5867	30	63
T63.62:5870	49	92
T64.7:5989	73	105
T64.8:5990	13	45
T64.10:6013	72	105
T64.15:6065	82	110
T64.28:6355	50	93
T64.30:6362	55	94
T64.32:6367	71	104
T64.33:6368	40	78
T64.40:6393	54	94
T64.43:6499	77	107
T64.44:6514	83	111
T65.2:6627	16	47
T65.5:6637	61	96
T65.9:6691	26	58
T65.10:6722	68	103
T65.11:6740	62	96

Inventory Number	Catalogue Number	Figure Number
T65.13:6810	31	64, 65, 66
T65.18:6857	67	100, 101
T67.12:7440	42	83
T68.17:7830	20	52
T68.19:7854	90	116
T69.8:8016	97	
T70.3:8093	66	99
T72.1:8192	80	
T74.1:8300	7	38

Non-excavated pieces from the area of Sardis

Inventory Number	Catalogue Number	Figure Number
NoEx 60.5	29	62
NoEx 65.1	56	95
NoEx 71.16	5	35, 36
NoEx 71.17	81	109
NoEx 72.5	37	75
NoEx 73.3	3	30
NoEx 73.6	23	54

Uninventoried pieces

Inventory Number	Catalogue Number	Figure Number
Chance find 1960	32	67
HoB 1963	101	123
PN 1965	100	119, 120, 121, 122

INDEX

ILLUSTRATIONS

Unless otherwise indicated, the scales used with objects are divided into one centimeter units, those on plans into one meter units. The measure used in field shots is one meter divided into ten centimeter units.

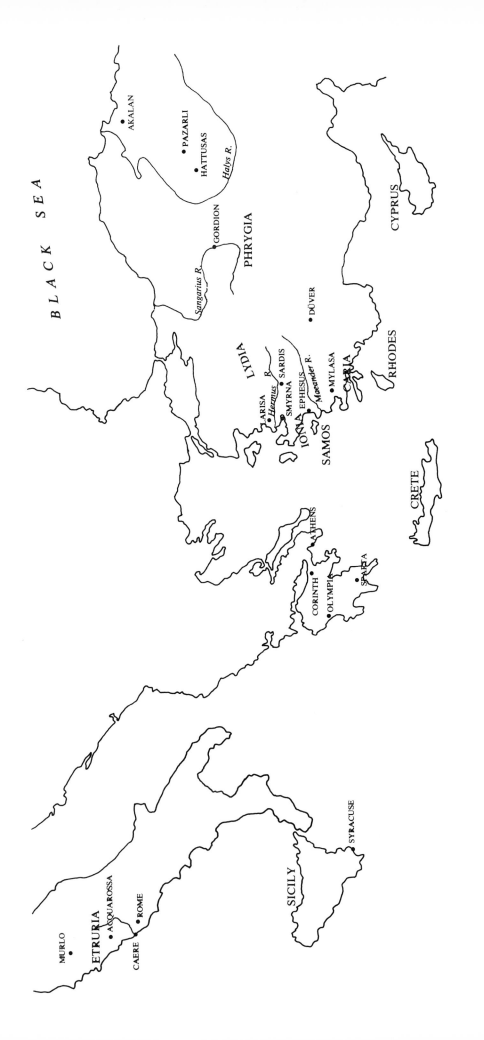

Fig. 1 Map of Aegean and Asia Minor.

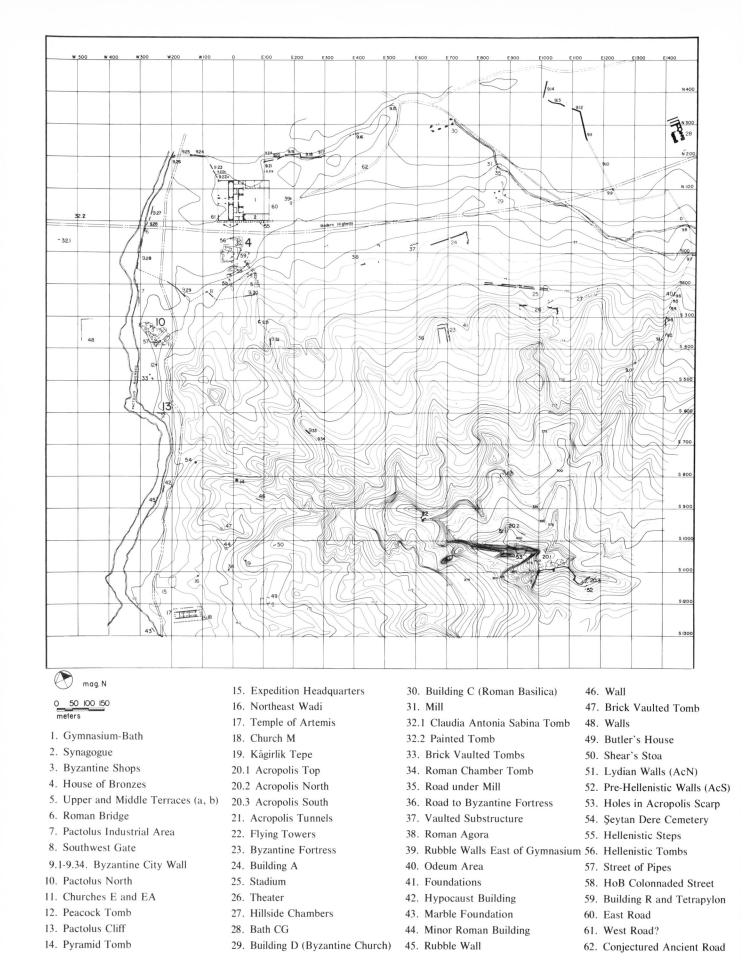

mag. N

0 50 100 150
meters

1. Gymnasium-Bath
2. Synagogue
3. Byzantine Shops
4. House of Bronzes
5. Upper and Middle Terraces (a, b)
6. Roman Bridge
7. Pactolus Industrial Area
8. Southwest Gate
9.1-9.34. Byzantine City Wall
10. Pactolus North
11. Churches E and EA
12. Peacock Tomb
13. Pactolus Cliff
14. Pyramid Tomb

15. Expedition Headquarters
16. Northeast Wadi
17. Temple of Artemis
18. Church M
19. Kâgirlik Tepe
20.1 Acropolis Top
20.2 Acropolis North
20.3 Acropolis South
21. Acropolis Tunnels
22. Flying Towers
23. Byzantine Fortress
24. Building A
25. Stadium
26. Theater
27. Hillside Chambers
28. Bath CG
29. Building D (Byzantine Church)

30. Building C (Roman Basilica)
31. Mill
32.1 Claudia Antonia Sabina Tomb
32.2 Painted Tomb
33. Brick Vaulted Tombs
34. Roman Chamber Tomb
35. Road under Mill
36. Road to Byzantine Fortress
37. Vaulted Substructure
38. Roman Agora
39. Rubble Walls East of Gymnasium
40. Odeum Area
41. Foundations
42. Hypocaust Building
43. Marble Foundation
44. Minor Roman Building
45. Rubble Wall

46. Wall
47. Brick Vaulted Tomb
48. Walls
49. Butler's House
50. Shear's Stoa
51. Lydian Walls (AcN)
52. Pre-Hellenistic Walls (AcS)
53. Holes in Acropolis Scarp
54. Şeytan Dere Cemetery
55. Hellenistic Steps
56. Hellenistic Tombs
57. Street of Pipes
58. HoB Colonnaded Street
59. Building R and Tetrapylon
60. East Road
61. West Road?
62. Conjectured Ancient Road

Fig. 2 Site plan with excavations and ruins of Sardis. The principle Lydian sectors are Nos. 4, 10, 13.

Fig. 3 PN, overall plan of main Lydian levels. The numbers refer to units.

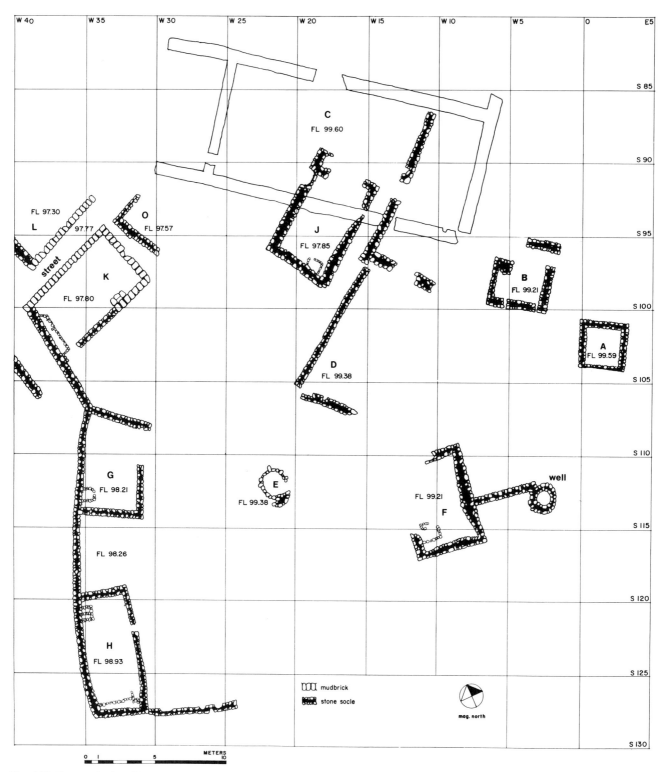

Fig. 4 HoB, overall plan of main Lydian levels.

Fig. 5 Sart Mustafa, general view of village houses.

Fig. 6 Lydian wall and floors in units 1 and 2 (at left) in PN.

Fig. 7 Northeast corner of unit 1.

Fig. 8 Half-built house near Sardis.

Fig. 9 PN, decorative stonework at southeast corner of unit 24.

Fig. 10 PN, ''herringbone'' wall of unit 23.

Fig. 11 HoB, unit L plastered wall and indication of windows.

Fig. 12 Sart Mustafa, modern pisé wall.

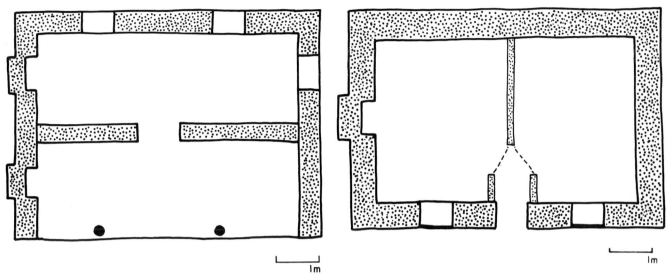

Fig. 13 Generalized plan of house in Sart Mustafa.

Fig. 14 Plan of late eighteenth century house in Tobermory, Scotland.

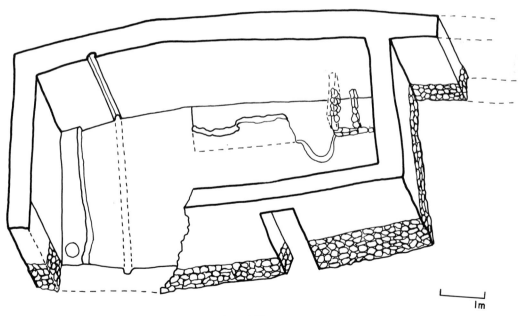

Fig. 15 HoB, isometric reconstruction drawing of H.

Fig. 16 HoB, detail of mud brick in H.

Fig. 17 Barn in Sart Mustafa
with pitched earth roof.

Fig. 18 Lydian bread tray.

Fig. 19 PN, unit 28 looking northwest.

Fig. 20 PN, detail of
doorway in unit 28.

Fig. 21 PN, unit 1 and 2 overall.

Fig. 22 PN, unit 1 from east.

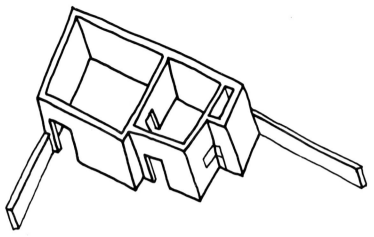

Fig. 23 PN, isometric sketch of units 1, 1a, and 2.

Fig. 24 HoB, roofing fragments of Bronze Age hut.

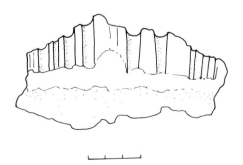

Figs. 25-26 HoB, seventh century roofing fragment.

Fig. 27 Sart Mustafa, house with friezelike row of bricks under the eaves.

Fig. 28 Side views of **6** (T60.30).

Fig. 29 Striations on the back of **27** (T61.61).

Fig. 30 **1** and **3**

Fig. 31 **1**

Fig. 32 **1** detail.

Fig. 33 **2**

Fig. 34 **4**

Fig. 35 **5**

Fig. 36 **5** reconstruction.

Fig. 37 **6**

Fig. 38 **7**

Fig. 39 **8**

Fig. 40 **9**

Fig. 41 **10**

Fig. 42 **11**

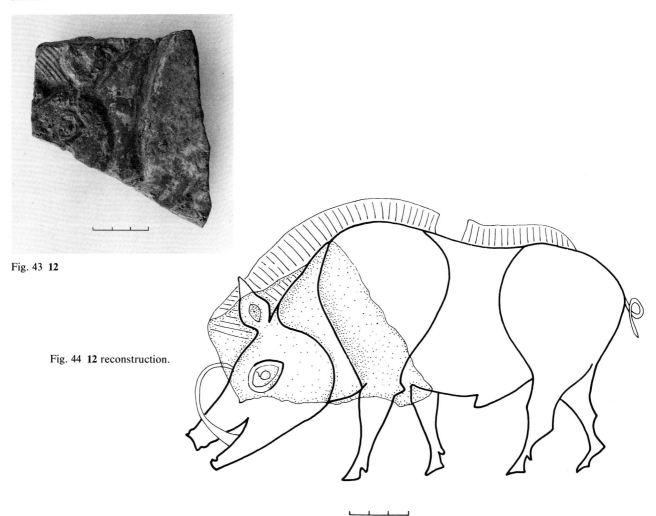

Fig. 43 **12**

Fig. 44 **12** reconstruction.

Fig. 45 **13**

Fig. 46 **14**

Fig. 47 **15** and **16,** taken from the same mold.

Fig. 48 **17**

Fig. 49 **18**

Fig. 50 **19**

Fig. 51 Recreated sima based on **19** and **42.**

Fig. 52 **20**

Fig. 53 **21** and **22** from the same mold and possibly the same frieze.

Fig. 54 **23**

Fig. 55 **24**

Fig. 56 **24** reconstruction.

Fig. 57 **25**

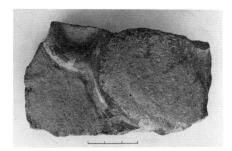

Fig. 58 **26**

Fig. 59 **27**

Figs. 60-61 **28** and reconstruction drawing.

Fig. 62 **29**

Fig. 63 **30**

Fig. 64 **31**

Fig. 65 **31**

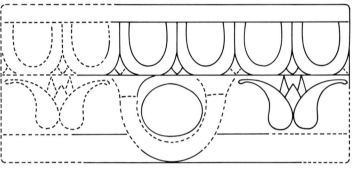

Fig. 66 **31** restored front view.

Fig. 67 **32**

Fig. 68 **33**

Fig. 69 **33** underside.

Fig. 70 **34**

Fig. 71 **35**

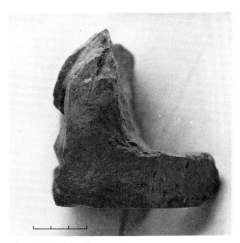

Fig. 72 **35** side view.

Fig. 73 **36**

Fig. 74 **36** profile.

Fig. 75 **37**

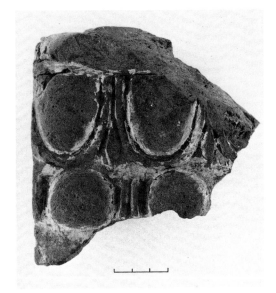

Fig. 76 **38**

Fig. 77 **39**

Fig. 78 **40**

Fig. 79 **41** front face.

Fig. 80 **41** underside.

Fig. 81 **41** roughened face.

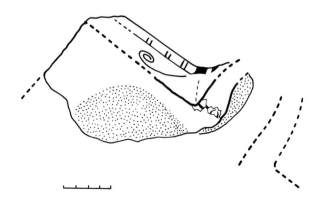

Fig. 82 **41** drawing showing restored view from above.

Fig. 83 **42**

Figs. 84-85 Plastic vase in form of a hare (P67.78) and fragment of Corinthian aryballos (P67.140) found with **42**.

Fig. 86 **43**   Fig. 87 **44**

Fig. 88 **45**

Fig. 89 **46**

Fig. 90 **47**

Fig. 91 **48**

Fig. 92 **49**

Fig. 93 **50**

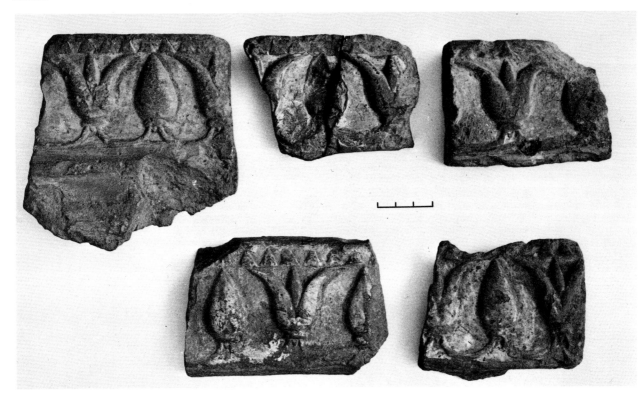

Fig. 94 Top: **51–53.** Bottom: **54** and **55.**

Fig. 95 **56–58**

Fig. 96 **59–62**

Fig. 97 **63** and **64**

Fig. 98 **65**

Fig. 99 **66**

Fig. 100 **67**

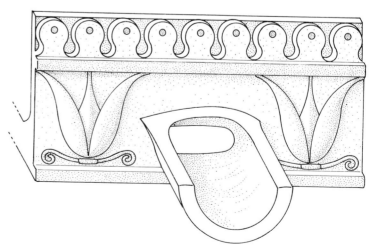

Fig. 101 **67** reconstruction.

1a

1b

Fig. 102 Main types of antefix.

2a

2b

3

4

Fig. 103 **68**

Fig. 104 **69–71**

Fig. 105 Top: **72** and **73.** Bottom: **74.**

Fig. 106 **75**

Fig. 107 **76, 77, 79**

Fig. 108 **78**

Fig. 109 **81**

Fig. 110 **82**

Fig. 111 **83**

Fig. 112 **86**

Fig. 113 **87**

Fig. 114 **88**

Fig. 115 **89**

Fig. 116 **90**

Fig. 117 **91** and **93**

Fig. 118 Top: **95** and **96.** Bottom: **99.**

Fig. 119 **100**

Fig. 120 **100** back.

Fig. 121 **100** side.

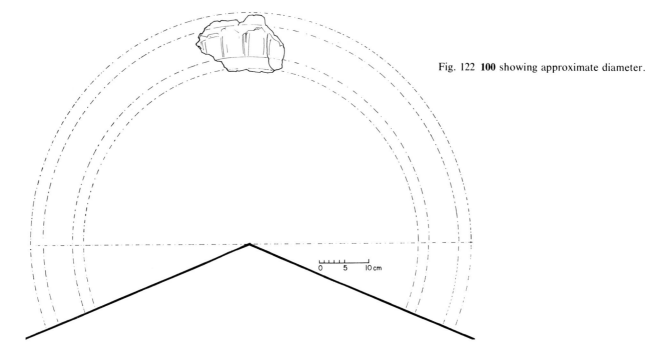

Fig. 122 **100** showing approximate diameter.

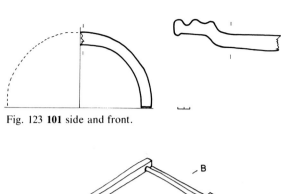

Fig. 123 **101** side and front.

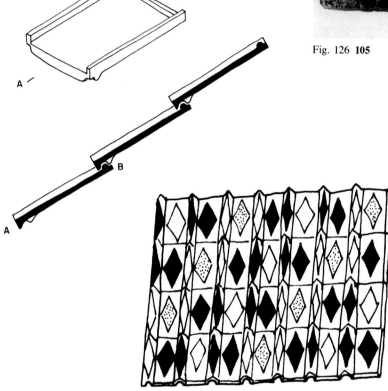

Fig. 126 **105**

Fig. 127 **106**

Fig. 124 Pantile linkage system and diamond pattern (the shaded diamonds represent red with the black and white).

Fig. 125 Top: **102.** Bottom: **103** and **104.**

Fig. 128 **107**

Fig. 129 **108**

Fig. 130 Shoulder and body fragment from Orientalizing amphora (P69.71) from NEW.

Fig. 131 Top of Lydian grave stele (NoEx 73.1).

Fig. 132 Lydian column crater (P69.56) from NEW.